The Mitchell Beazley pocket guide to
Cheese

Sandy Carr

Mitchell Beazley

Key to symbols

see p. 8

🐄 cows' milk

🐑 ewes' milk

🐐 goats' milk

see p. 10

very soft

soft

semisoft

semihard

hard

see p. 10

○ sphere

⬭ drum

▱ rectangular loaf

⊖ wheel

▭ square

⬭ roll

N.B. Shape applies to whole cheese

🍎 used in cooking

Ⓐ widely available

Ⓑ outside country of origin available only in specialist shops

Ⓒ widely available in country of origin

Ⓓ rare or difficult to find outside area of production

★ recommended for excellence and/or interest

Fat content is shown as a percentage (see p. 10) and the approximate weight of a whole cheese is given in both kg and lb

Edited and designed by
Mitchell Beazley Publishers
87–89 Shaftesbury Avenue, London W1V 7AD
© Mitchell Beazley Publishers 1981
All rights reserved
ISBN 0 85533 359 6

Typeset by Servis Filmsetting Ltd, Manchester, UK
Printed in Hong Kong by Mandarin Offset International Ltd

Editor Bobbi Mitchell
Designer Jacquie Gulliver
Map illustrator Eugene Fleury
Editor in Chief Susannah Read
Art Editor Douglas Wilson
Production Julian Deeming

Contents

Introduction

Cheese, according to the ancient Greeks, was a gift from the gods. This may have been another way of saying that nobody could really remember when, where or how it first came into being, or perhaps, unaware of the chemical processes involved, the Greeks believed there was something miraculous about the transformation of milk into cheese. Like transmuting base metal into gold, it was something beyond the skill of mere mortals, and required the intervention of a divine being.

The true origins of cheesemaking are, and probably always will be, a mystery. Like many inventions, cheese was probably discovered by different peoples simultaneously. Once they had realized that the milk of certain mammals was both appetizing and nutritious, it was but a short step to the observation that sour milk separates naturally into curds and whey, and from there to cheesemaking. Herds of sheep and cattle were raised for milking in Sumeria and ancient Egypt, sheep were domesticated in Mesopotamia about 12,000 years ago and in the Old Testament there are many references to ewes' and cows' milk cheeses. Classical Greek literature provides abundant evidence that by that time, cheesemaking had long passed the primitive stage. Even in those days cheese was made not only for domestic use but for trade. Recent excavations have uncovered evidence of a cheese market in Jerusalem and a cheese factory in northern Israel, and by the 6th century BC the Romans were importing cheese from all over the Empire.

Then, as now, cheese was prized not only as a staple food (often being, for the peasant, the only form of protein in an otherwise frugal diet) but also as a delicacy worthy of the attention of the most exigent gastronome. Cheese was, and is, all things to all men. It can be robust or delicate, strong or soothing, an abundant meal in itself or a rare and precious morsel to be savoured, cosseted and treated with the reverence afforded all great miracles of art or nature.

This book seeks to demonstrate above all that *cheese is not one thing*. There are hundreds, maybe thousands, of different cheeses. Some of them are widely available, others only within a few miles of the locality in which they are made. Yet although more and more cheeses are being sold by cheesemongers everywhere, we often stick to old favourites and shy away from trying something new. Confused by the choice confronting us, we fall back on the tried and trusty—Cheddar, Brie, Camembert, Edam, Danablu, possibly a little Emmental or Gruyère, or for the more adventurous, some Gorgonzola, Roquefort or Taleggio. This is like reading the same half-dozen books over and over again and ignoring the rest of the library. What we need is a little knowledge to inform our choice and a degree of encouragement to help us over the brink. This book aims to provide both.

I have chosen over 1,200 cheeses from all over the world, some of which will already be familiar to you, others mere acquaintances and some complete strangers. The main characteristics of each with regard to taste, texture, etc., are described, together with any idiosyncrasies of temperament. Cheeses can be notoriously temperamental and a chance encounter with a bad one can lead to lifelong antipathy. It is therefore important to know how to tell a good cheese from a bad one and how, having found it, to cherish it.

Cheesemaking processes

The simple milk-to-cheese formula has endless possibilities, depending partly on the milk itself and partly on the processing by the cheesemaker.

By the time the milk leaves the animal, a host of factors has already determined the nature of the cheese to some extent. The nature of the grazing—whether fresh grass or scrub, hay, clover, corn or manufactured concentrates—influences milk yield and flavour. Climate and even microorganisms present in the air also have a part to play. The animal itself—be it cow, sheep, goat, buffalo, camel, yak, zebu or reindeer—will be a major influence on the eventual cheese. Each cheese type is based on a unique combination of all these factors even before man begins his work. For this reason it is notoriously difficult to reproduce some cheeses outside their area of origin. It also explains why and how some expert cheese tasters can identify not only the area but even the specific farm where a particular cheese was produced (provided it is made from unpasteurized milk).

Pasteurization is a means of partially sterilizing milk to destroy potentially harmful bacteria and makes it possible to mix milk from different herds to allow for large-scale industrialized cheesemaking. But in doing so, some cheese connoisseurs and cheesemakers would argue, it also destroys much of the individuality of the cheese and makes for a blander product. It is to unpasteurized cheese what 'plonk' is to vintage wine. Nevertheless, most of the cows' milk cheese made in the world today is made from pasteurized milk (ewes' and goats' milk is rarely pasteurized). Some countries (for instance, the United States and Denmark) impose a blanket ban on unpasteurized cheese, which is unfortunate since it is almost always fuller in flavour than the same cheese made from pasteurized milk. Unpasteurized cheese made in modern dairies is not a health hazard. Standards of hygiene and quality control have improved immeasurably in recent years and besides, most of the pathogens present in milk are destroyed by the cheesemaking process itself.

The basic principles of cheesemaking are the same for all cheeses. The object is to extract the water from the milk, leaving the milk solids (fat, protein, vitamins, etc.) behind. To simplify the stages of a very complex process, this involves coagulating the milk, treating the curds, moulding, pressing and finishing the cheese and then leaving it to ripen. There are of course many variations at each stage which all contribute to the nature of the final cheese.

Coagulating the milk

The cheesemaker may choose to use morning milk, evening milk or a mixture of the two. It may then be partly or fully skimmed or more cream may be added. At this moment the cheesemaker may add a dye (such as annatto) or mould spores (such as *Pencillium roquefortii*) to promote veining, or propionic acid bacteria to encourage the development of holes. The milk is brought up to a uniform temperature (varying from cheese to cheese) and soured by means of a starter (a special culture of sour milk with a high concentration of lactic acid). From now on, until salt is added at a later stage, the acidity of the curds will gradually rise. The cheesemaker tests the level constantly so that he knows when it is time to move on to the next stage. Some cheeses are coagulated entirely by lactic acid and are known as lactic-curd or acid-curd cheeses. Others require rennet, an enzyme extracted from the stomach of a young calf (or lamb). When the levels of acidity and temperature are right (they vary for each cheese), the rennet is added, causing a reaction in the milk that separates it into curds and whey. At one time, plant rennets such as the juice of fig leaves, thistle seeds, safflower, melon and ladies' bedstraw (*caille-lait* in French) were widely used. They still are for cheeses made specifically for vegetarians, in kosher cheese and in some Asian types where religious beliefs forbid the eating of cow's meat. Some countries, notably Portugal, still use plant rennets to make many of their traditional cheese types. After renneting, the milk gradually forms one huge mass of junket.

Treating the curds

The curds are next cut and drained. The size of the cut, the method used and the amount of time expended will determine the moisture content and consequently the softness or hardness of the cheese. For softer cheeses the curds are sparingly cut and ladled into moulds to drain naturally. For harder cheeses the curds are cut vertically and horizontally into tiny pieces, or combed into fine strands. As the curds settle on the bottom of the vat, they may be recut and turned (pitched) or piled in blocks one on top of the other (cheddared) to expel the maximum amount of whey. Sometimes, as in the case of very hard cheeses, the curds are 'cooked' in the whey before being drained, in that the vat is heated to bring the curds up to a specific temperature. For some semi-hard cheeses the temperature of the vat is also raised, but less high, so that the curds are 'scalded' rather than 'cooked'. Some cheese types also involve the addition of herbs or spices or wine to the curds during this stage.

One important variation in the treatment of curd is that instanced by many Italian cheeses and known in Italy as *pasta filata* and elsewhere as spun-curd or plastic-curd cheeses. The drained curd is immersed in hot water, where it becomes soft and pliable, and then stretched and kneaded until it reaches the required consistency. The whey drained from the curd can be heated (to collect residual milk proteins and fats, etc.) and used to make another cheese, as in the case of Ricotta, Mysost and Broccio, which are all whey cheeses. Albumen cheese (such as Sapsago) is made by heating whole or skimmed milk and is very rare.

Moulding, pressing, finishing

At this stage the cheesemaking process splinters and veers off in several directions and the more obvious visual differences between cheeses begin to emerge. The curds, once treated in the appropriate way, are spooned, ladled or shovelled into moulds of a vast range of shapes and sizes, perforated to complete drainage. The moulds may be stainless steel drums, wooden hoops or rush baskets or any other suitable vessels. The curds may be left to firm naturally or they may be pressed, either lightly or heavily. Alternatively the curds may be scooped out of the vat in a cheesecloth and moulded by hand.

The cheese is then often subjected to other processes. It may be soaked in brine, be bandaged or waxed, be sprayed with mould-forming spores or exposed to bacteria. It may be washed with water, brine or alcohol, or buried in ashes or herbs, oiled or painted, smoked, or even just left alone to ripen in its own way.

Ripening

This is the last critical stage in cheesemaking. Its length varies with each cheese type—from four weeks or so for soft cheese like Camembert to two or three years for Parmesan. Fresh cheeses are barely ripened at all. Even within the same cheese type the period of ripening can vary considerably. This means that the process must be carefully monitored throughout by expert cheese graders who are specifically attuned to the qualities of each cheese. The colour, shape, texture, aroma and even the sound of a cheese all indicate whether or not it is à point. In some cases the grader 'irons' the cheese: a long, thin, metal cylinder—the cheese iron—is inserted into the centre of the cheese and pulled out, bringing a rod of cheese with it. The colour, smell and texture are examined before it is replaced in the cheese. The Cheshire cheese grader will also hold it to his ear, listening for minute squelching sounds which tell him that there is too much or too little moisture in the cheese. The Parmesan grader thumps the cheese and listens to the vibrations coming from the crust. Each cheese is tested in different ways.

During the ripening period the conditions of temperature and humidity are carefully controlled to promote the development of desirable micro-organisms which help the process and discourage those that hinder it. Some cheeses are ripened from the inside out, while others are ripened from the outside in. For some, the object is to encourage internal moulds, for others to prevent them. All these require different conditions in the cheese store.

It is during the ripening period that special characteristics develop, like the blue veining in Stilton, the holes in Emmental, the red smear on the surface of Liederkrantz and the white mould on a Camembert. This sometimes happens naturally, but there is usually something the cheesemaker can do to help it along. For example, by piercing the cheese with fine stainless steel needles, the cheesemaker can aerate the paste and so help the veins in blue cheeses spread. By turning a holey cheese regularly, the cheesemaker ensures that the holes will be evenly formed and distributed throughout the cheese. In earlier days, the proper development of these characteristics depended not only on the cheesemaker but also to a large extent on luck. Nowadays the cheesemaker's skill is still essential, but very little is left to chance. What was once a domestic art has now become a fully fledged thriving industry.

Classification of cheese

The sheer multiplicity of cheese types is, at first sight, quite bewildering. It is rather like being introduced to a huge crowd of people who, although all recognizably human, are each individuals in their own right. Yet, like humans, cheeses can be grouped in various ways, so converting the complexity to manageable proportions. Individual cheeses will fall into different groups depending on the method of classification used.

This guide to cheese represents one way in which cheese can be classified—by country of origin. As far as possible, cheeses have been assigned to their country of origin, even though, in many cases, they are made in several other countries as well. Cheese is closely related to climatic, geographical, economic and cultural circumstances. Some people even perceive national characteristics that make one nation's cheeses different as a whole from another's. Other forms of classification relate to the nature of the processing, the type of milk used, texture, fat content, shape, size, colour, flavour, smell and type of rind.

Processing

The various permutations of the cheesemaking process allow a rough and ready classification along the following lines:

Fresh cheeses unripened or barely ripened cheeses coagulated with rennet (rennet-curd) or by lactic fermentation (acid- or lactic-curd). Some may be lightly pressed or moulded by hand, but mostly they are simply packed into tubs or crocks.

Ripened unpressed cheeses curds are minimally cut and allowed to drain naturally. Quick-ripened (about a month) by surface moulds. Includes cheeses with white rind flora and those with orange to brown washed rinds.

Pressed uncooked cheeses lightly or heavily pressed and medium-ripened (from two to 18 months).

Pressed cooked cheeses curds are 'cooked' in the whey before being moulded, heavily pressed and ripened up to four years.

Pasta filata cheeses curd is immersed in hot water, kneaded and moulded (often by hand). Ripened or unripened.

Whey cheeses usually made as a by-product of other cheeses. May be fresh, pressed and dried, or caramelized.

Processed cheeses made by blending one or more natural cheeses with various other ingredients including vegetable oils, butter, emulsifiers, artificial preservatives and flavourings. Such cheeses or rather cheese products are outside the scope of this book.

Type of milk

Milk may be whole, or partly or fully skimmed, and this affects the fat content of the cheese. It may also be pasteurized or unpasteurized (see previous chapter). The flavour of the cheese is determined, above all, by the type of animal that provides the milk. In some cases, even the particular breed is significant, much as grape variety is in winemaking.

Cows' milk cheeses most of the world's cheeses are made from cows' milk. The lactation period of dairy cattle is unusually long: up to ten months in some cases, followed by a two-month dry period. By staggering calf production in a large herd, milk can be made available all year round. The milk changes in character and reduces in yield during the lactation period. The first milk produced after calving is a rich concentrated substance called colostrum or beestings. This is full of nourishment for the newborn calf, but rarely used in cheesemaking. It is followed by the 'new' milk, high in fats and proteins. Both the yield and the fat content gradually reduce until the end of the lactation period, when the milk increases in fats once again. Milk produced towards the end of a milking is also higher in fats than the first flow. (Some cheeses, such as Reblochon, are traditionally made only from this milk.) Cows are milked twice a day, evening and morning. Most cheeses are made of a mixture of the two milkings, but they can also be used separately or sometimes coagulated separately and then mixed. The fodder and nature of grazing also affect the milk and thence the cheese. Legal controls specify exactly what the cows may be fed on in many cases. Cheeses made from summer milk are generally regarded as superior.

Ewes' milk cheeses sheep can thrive in harsh conditions and on pasture that would be quite unsuitable for cattle. The lactation period is short and the yield low, but the use of ewes' milk enables cheesemaking to take place in areas where it would not otherwise be possible. Some countries, notably Spain, Portugal, Pyrenean France and parts of Italy are particularly renowned for their ewes' milk cheeses. Unlike cows' milk, the availability of ewes' milk is highly seasonal. The precise limits depend on climate, latitude and on certain local conditions—in France, for example, the season lasts from about January to mid-May. Fresh cheeses are found only in these months. The availability of ewes' milk cheeses depends on the length of the ripening period. Three-month ripened cheeses are available from April to mid-August. Ewes' milk cheeses are almost always sharper than cows' milk cheeses.

Goats' milk cheeses goats' milk is exceptionally high in fat content and is free from many of the pathogens that affect cows' milk—one reason why it is hardly ever pasteurized. Goats have a high milk yield and can live on difficult terrain, but their lactation period is short and the milk, therefore, seasonal. Pure goats' milk cheeses are available from the beginning of spring to the end of autumn. Otherwise they are likely to be mixed cows' and goats' milk cheeses. Goats' cheeses should have a stronger, fuller barnyard flavour than any others.

Other animals cheese is rarely made nowadays from the milk of other animals. Yaks', reindeers' and camels' milk cheeses do still exist in some remote areas. The water buffalo is more important, particularly in Italy and the Balkans, but even there it is being supplanted by the more amenable cow.

Texture

The hardness or softness of a cheese is directly related to its moisture content. The harder the cheese the lower the moisture content. The world of cheese is a continuum between very soft and very hard so that any classification is likely to be arbitrary, especially where one group shades into the next. Also, many cheeses lose moisture as they mature. A four-year-old Parmesan is much harder than a two-year-old one. With these reservations, most cheeses fall into one or other of the following groups:

Very soft spoonable cheeses. Most fresh cheeses come into this category but not all (such as Mozzarella).

Soft spreadable cheeses like Camembert or Brie.

Semisoft firmer, often crumbly or springy but still moist. Many blues and Trappist cheeses come into this category.

Semihard the largest family and what the Germans call *Schnittkäse* (sliceable cheese), such as Cheshire, Tilsit.

Hard very firm, dense, sometimes grainy cheeses. Sliceable when young and grated when old, like Parmesan, Cheddar, Sbrinz.

Fat content

An important indicator of the overall food value of a cheese. Vitamins A and D are both fat-soluble so the higher the fat content the greater the concentration of these vitamins in the cheese. High fat cheeses should be avoided by people on low cholesterol diets. Fat content is also related in part to the calorific value of cheese. Generally, the higher the fat, the higher the calories. Fat content is always expressed as a minimum percentage of the dry matter, ignoring the moisture content, which varies with age. This means that the *actual* fat content for a given weight of a high moisture cheese will be lower than for the same weight of a low moisture cheese. Camembert and Emmental have the same fat content (45 per cent) but 100g (3½oz) of Emmental will contain more fat than the same amount of Camembert because Emmental contains less moisture.

Shape and size

Cheeses come in many shapes and sizes. These may be a result of tradition, or the aesthetic preference of the cheesemaker or even just of marketing convenience. Often, however, they are directly related to the nature of the cheese and to the ripening process in particular. A Camembert, for example, has to be small and flattish with a large surface area in relation to its volume. If it were not, the surface micro-organisms would not penetrate to the centre before the outside became overripe. Similarly, the convex sides characteristic of many cheeses are a result of gases given off during fermentation. Six basic shapes predominate; sphere, drum, rectangular loaf, wheel or disc, square or cube, roll or sausage. Cheeses listed in this book have been assigned to one of these groups wherever possible, and variations on the norm explained wherever applicable. In all cases, it is the traditional shape of the whole cheese that has been cited. Many cheeses nowadays are also available in easily sliceable rectangular blocks.

Colour

Natural cheeses range in colour from white through all the shades of yellow to dark chocolate brown. Their colour generally depends on the length of the ripening process combined with the butter-fat content of the milk. It deepens during ripening and the richer the original milk, the more golden the cheese. This is, however, complicated by the fact that artificial colouring agents are also used. The most common is annatto (*Bixa orellana*), a plant of West Indian origin, responsible for the deep orange colour characteristic of some cheeses. In the past, saffron, carrot juice and marigold petals were used for the same purpose. Some cheeses, such as Feta, are bleached. Sapsago gets its green colour from powdered blue melilot.

Flavour and smell

Cheeses range from mild to strong in both flavour and smell but the precise nuances depend as much on the person doing the tasting or smelling as on the cheese itself. The following descriptions can only therefore be a rough guide. Taste before you buy wherever possible. Smelly cheeses, by the way, are not necessarily strong tasting.

Rind

The rind of a cheese is usually very distinctive. Although fresh cheeses generally have no rind at all, most cheeses fall into one of four groups: dry natural rind, soft bloomy white rind, yellow-red washed rind or artificial rind.

Dry natural rinds formed by the curds at the edges of the cheese drying out. They may be brushed or bandaged to make them coarse or grainy or they may be oiled to become smooth and shiny. Generally tough, hard and thick.

Soft bloomy white rinds have a thin or thick growth of white mould on the surface. *Penicillium candidum* is sprayed on the soft moulded curds and the resultant growth of white fur is regularly brushed off until the desired thickness of rind is achieved. Pure white and dry to touch when the cheese is fresh, darkening with age. The rind may or may not be eaten.

Washed rinds cheeses washed with water, brine, wine or beer and sometimes a culture of *Breyibacterium linens* develop a smeary bacterial growth, which varies from yellow to dark red depending on the intensity of the treatment. Usually softish and damp to touch, often smelly. Rarely eaten.

Artificial rinds 'artificial' in that they do not arise from the cheese itself. The substance may be organic, such as herbs or leaves, or inorganic such as wax or ashes.

Africa

Most of Africa is totally unsuited to cheesemaking. Violent extremes of climate, and vegetation ranging from desert to jungle typify the bulk of the continent. Cattle are mostly of the zebu type whose already scant yield is not helped by the lack of adequate fodder in periods of drought. These animals were once important indicators of wealth and since they were beasts of burden they were not used for milk before the Europeans came. There were exceptions, notably the Masai, whose infamous blood and milk cocktails must have made up in nutritive value what they singularly lacked in aesthetic appeal. But except in the Islamic north there is no evidence that cheese formed a part of the native African diet. Colonial administrations introduced cheesemaking to those countries where conditions were favourable. Native cattle were crossed with European breeds and in South Africa and Kenya, for instance, there is now a thriving dairy industry producing, as yet, only copies of European cheeses. North African cheeses are generally ewes' or goats' milk types made by semi-nomadic herdsmen.

Aoules (Algeria)
Made from skimmed goats' milk sometimes diluted with water and using a piece of the previous cheese batch as a starter. The curds and whey are placed in an animal skin bag and shaken vigorously to produce lumps of butter fat. The remaining watery liquid is heated and the cloudy curds are moulded into small round cakes. These are dried in the sun until hard and flinty, pulverized and then used for seasoning.

Jbane (Morocco)
Goats' or sometimes cows' milk coagulated with vegetable or animal rennet, drained in woven rush bowls, moulded into discs and dried. Sometimes eaten fresh.

Numidia (Tunisia)
Potent blue-veined cheese made from ewes' or goats' milk.

Oriental (Tunisia)
White brined ewes' milk cheese similar to Greek Feta.

Sarde (Tunisia)
Pressed, uncooked ewes' milk cheese like Spanish Manchego.

Sicille (Tunisia)
Semi-hard white cheese with lots of holes made from ewes' milk mixed with a little cows' or goats' milk. Eaten young after one to three months ripening, or aged up to a year.

Takammart (Algeria)
Made with whole goats' milk started with a chunk of the previous batch. The curds are drained first on straw mats and then kneaded. Roughly moulded into small flat squares and left to dry in the sun for two to three days. Stored in goatskin bags until hard and brittle. Once used as money.

Testouri (Tunisia)
Hand-moulded balls of fresh ewes' or goats' milk curds.

ARGENTINA see *Latin America*

Asia

Few Asian countries make any cheeses of note. Many make none at all. The Chinese still regard milk as a repulsive substance quite unfit for human consumption. The Japanese have no indigenous cheesemaking traditions although they now make some foreign types and are passionately fond of processed cheese. Such Asian cheeses as do exist are mostly fairly primitive fresh types. The controlled conditions necessary to ripen cheese successfully present insuperable problems in tropical climates where refrigeration is still relatively uncommon.

Aarey (India)
Semi-hard buffalo milk cheese made near Bombay.

Bandal (India)
Acid-curd cheese made from whole milk or cream. Shaped into small balls and eaten fresh, or smoked over wood or dung fires. Made in West Bengal from cows' or buffalo milk.

Chauna, Chhana (India)
Acid-curd cows' milk cheese eaten fresh or used in sweetmeats.

Chura (Tibet)
Yaks' milk is a staple of the Tibetan nomads. It is made into butter and *ghee*, an all-purpose oil. Cheese of a kind is also made although it is not coagulated in the normal way. This one is sour buttermilk, heated, drained, moulded into balls and hung up to dry. It is used for grating.

Dacca (India)
Made from cows' or buffalo milk or a mixture of the two. Drained in wicker or bamboo baskets and pressed. Dried for about two weeks and then smoked.

Karut, Krut, Kurt
The nomadic tribesmen of central Asia were certainly among the first cheesemakers. Yet technological advances require settled habits and cheesemaking in that area today is still extraordinarily primitive. Krut is made in Pakistan, Iran, Afghanistan and by the Turkoman tribes of southern USSR, using any available milk. Made by boiling buttermilk and draining and drying the solids. Has to be reconstituted with water before being eaten but it will keep for years.

Kesong Puti (Philippines)
Fresh cheese made from buffalo milk. Wrapped in leaves.

Lighvan (Iran)
White brined cheese made from ewes', cows' or goats' milk.

Panir (Iran)
White goats' milk cheese.

Peshavani (India)
Ewes' or buffalo milk cheese coagulated with withania berries.

Surati Panir (India)
Buffalo milk cheese from Gujarat. The curds are drained and then ripened in whey for 12 to 36 hours. Sold in clay pots.

Australasia

AUSTRALIA

The early settlers in Australia found little in the way of agricultural traditions. Nearly two-thirds of the continent is composed of desert and barren scrublands, rich in mineral deposits but poor in pasture. The Aborigine population basically consisted of hunters and gatherers relying on game and wild fruits and vegetables for sustenance. Nevertheless, the modern Australian dairy industry, concentrated in Queensland and New South Wales, is highly productive and efficient, and apart from making enough dairy products to satisfy its own needs, Australia has found ready markets abroad, especially in the Far East.

Of the few cheeses recognized as Australian, the most important is Cheedam, an innocuous golden yellow rindless block inspired by Cheddar and Edam. Pasterello, also unique to Australia, was invented in Sydney by an Italian, Daniele Lostia, and is a rather delicate softish cheese with a high moisture content, somewhat reminiscent of Fontal although it is drained in wicker baskets like several other Italian cheeses. There is also a creamy blue-veined type ripened in foil and similar to Gorgonzola. The Italian connection is more evident in the making of rather good imitation Ricotta, Mozzarella, Provolone, Parmesan, Pepato and Romano. The British were, of course, the first to colonize Australia in large numbers and Cheddar is still the most widely produced and consumed cheese. It is sold 'mild' (three months old), 'semi-mature' (three to six months), 'mature' (six to 12 months) and 'vintage' (over 18 months). Cheddars can also be flavoured with cumin, garlic, bacon or port wine; 'smoked'; or, in the case of processed Cheddars, flavoured with spring onion, ham, ginger, curry, chilli and even peanuts. Cheshire is the only other English type, produced in Southbrook, Queensland, since 1964.

Other foreign cheeses catering for nostalgic immigrant communities include a rather salty Feta, a type of Emmental sold as 'Swiss', Gouda, Edam and Leiden, a copy of Maltese Gbejna, available plain or coated in peppercorns, and versions of Brie and Camembert. All these cheeses, whatever their original characteristics, are made only from pasteurized cows' milk.

NEW ZEALAND

The New Zealand climate is mild, temperate and ideal for cattle raising. Although much smaller than Australia, the country is more important as a cheese producer in terms of exports, which place it second only to the Netherlands. Most dairy farming is concentrated in North Island around Auckland and the main breed is Jersey cattle, whose superb milk, rich in butterfat, accounts for the exceptionally high quality of most New Zealand cheese. Only pasteurized cows' milk cheeses are made and of these the most important is Cheddar, available plain or variously flavoured. Also produced are Cheshire, Edam, Gouda, Gruyère, Danbo, Feta, Romano, Parmesan, Havarti, Colby, Monterey, Blue Vein and a cheese called Egmont, which is a cross between Cheddar and Gouda. Needless to say, there are endless processed varieties available on the market. There are no indigenous cheese types.

Austria

Austrian cheeses can be divided into three types: hard
cooked cheeses, influenced by Swiss cheesemakers and
particularly suited to the mountainous terrain, strong
pungent cheeses with red rind flora, and soft fresh curd
cheeses, which both have affinities with their German
neighbours. Liptauer, a savoury cheese spread much liked in
Austria, is of eastern European origin.

Gratz (Graz)
A hard, tangy, cows' milk cheese made in Styria.

Güssing   🗒 ◗   ▱ 2–4kg (4–9lb) 🌣
Mild sweetish cheese with a springy consistency and a golden
buttery paste made from partly skimmed milk.

Impérial Frischkäse
A fresh, white, faintly salty cows' milk cheese.

Jochberg
Tyrolean cheese made from mixed cows' and goats' milk.

Marienhofer   🗒 🌒   ▱ 0.5kg (18oz) 🌣
Limburger type made from partly skimmed evening milk
mixed with whole morning milk.

Mischlingkäse   🗒 ◗ 15–35%   ◒ 8–30kg (18–66lb) 🌣
A dark golden cheese with an orangey dry rind. It has a
pleasantly spicy aroma and a full-bodied sharpish flavour. The
paste is scattered with a few irregular holes. Made in the
mountains of western Austria.

Mondseer   🗒 🌒 45%   ◒ 1kg (2lb) 🌣
Firm, moist, buttery cheese with a few irregular eyes and a soft
dry rind. Also called Mondseer Schachtelkäse.

Mondseer Schlosskäse see *Schlosskäse*

Montafoner
A soft, fresh, acid-curd cheese flavoured with chopped herbs.

Olmützer Quargel
Ripened acid-curd cheese, hand-moulded into small flat discs
and flavoured with caraway seeds. Sharp and fairly pungent.
Translucent, greyish-yellow, rubbery paste.

Pinzgauer Bierkäse   🗒 ◗ 15%   ◒ 4–30kg (9–66lb) 🌣
A piquant washed-rind cheese made in Salzburg.

Schlosskäse   🗒 🌒 35–45%   ◒ 50g (1¾oz) 🌣
Rather mild washed-rind cheese made in northern Austria.

Tiroler Graukäse ★   🗒 🌒 45% ◒   ◗
A curious cheese made from pressed ripened sour-milk curds
washed with Penicillium moulds during the ripening period so
that the mould spreads from the surface inwards, sometimes
leaving the core unpenetrated. Has a tangy, rather sour flavour.

Topfen   🗒 🌒 10–50% 🍎 🌣
A fresh cheese used in many Austrian dishes.

Belgium

The reputation of Belgian cheeses tends to be overshadowed by that of its more famous cheesemaking neighbours, France and the Netherlands, and even its best-known cheese, Limburger, has been effectively appropriated by Germany. Many Belgian cheeses are closely related to French types, which is not surprising given that a substantial proportion of the population is of French ancestry. The quality of these cheeses is very high and only the best are allowed to be exported. Ironically, most Belgian cheese exports consist not of its indigenous cheeses but of excellent copies of foreign types: Cheddar goes to England, Asiago, Fontina, Montasio and Canestrato end up in Italy. Apart from these, Belgium also makes Gouda, Emmental, Brie, Camembert and, interestingly, Spanish Manchego. A new range of Belgian cheeses was being developed in 1980.

Boulette
There are various local types of Boulette (those from Namur, Huy, Charleroi and Romedenne are the best known and most widely available). All are small, soft, surface-ripened farmhouse cheeses moulded into cylinders, drums, rolls and balls and variously flavoured with herbs, rolled in crushed spices or wrapped in leaves. Fairly strident in flavour and aroma. Generically related to the Boulette of French Flanders.

Bouquet des Moines
A type of Boulette, small, shaped like a tall drum and with a light covering of white rind flora.

Broodkaas
'Loaf cheese', rectangular block similar to Dutch Gouda, waxed red or orange. Smooth consistency, 40 per cent fat.

Brusselsekaas ★   🌡 ⏳ 15–20% 160g (5½oz) 🧀
Smooth, salty, low-fat cheese made from pasteurized skimmed milk. Regularly washed with tepid water during the three-month ripening period. It has virtually no rind and is moulded into small irregularly shaped cakes and packed in cellophane for sale. Fairly strong and tangy with a light spicy aroma. Also called Fromage de Bruxelles, Hettekees.

Cassette de Beaumont
Smooth, pale, creamy cheese moulded into a rough rectangular shape. A type of Boulette flavoured with salt and pepper. Sometimes sold in small willow baskets.

Fromage de Bruxelles see *Brusselsekaas*

Fromage Mou see *Macquée*

Fromage de Trappiste
Semi-hard cheese factory-made from pasteurized milk and inspired by Port-Salut and other French monastery cheeses. There are numerous types variously shaped into flat wheels or loaves and with smooth springy rinds ranging from light golden yellow to black. Often sold as 'Saint-Paulin' or under brand names such as Echte Loo, Vieille Abbaye, Perrette, Nouvelle Abbaye, Abbaye de la Vallée, Père Joseph and Paterskop. Mild and sometimes spiced.

Hertog van Brabant
Creamy, semi-hard cows' milk cheese similar to Saint-Bernard.

Herve ★   ⚄ ☽ 45% � 50–200g (1¾–7oz) ‹
Generic term for a family of strong pungent cheeses, of which
Remoudou is the best known, deriving from the town of Herve
in northern Liège. It is a washed-rind cheese dating back at least
to the mid-16th century. Its warm golden crust covers a rich
velvety paste ranging from sweet to spicy depending on the
length of the ripening period (two to three months). Traditional drinks with Herve cheese are coffee or port.

Hettekees see *Brusselsekaas*

Kampanjebrood op stro
Literally 'country loaf on straw'. A semi-hard cows' milk
cheese, mellow-flavoured, sold on a straw mat.

Limburger see *Germany, Federal Republic (Limburger)*

Macquée
Soft fresh cows' milk cheese made from partly skimmed milk.
Usually brick-shaped. Also called Fromage Mou.

Maredsous
Type of Saint-Paulin, rectangular with a white powdery rind.

Plateau   ⚄ ☽ 45% ⌔ 2·5kg (5½lb) ‹
Larger, milder, firmer member of the Herve family.

Plattekaas
Fresh curd cheese with a 20 to 40 per cent fat content.

Prince Jean
Type of Boulette available in several versions: unripened (*vers*),
ripened with white surface moulds (*geaffineerd*), or rolled in
crushed black peppercorns (*met peper*).

Remoudou ★   ⚄ ☽ 45% ⌔ 200g (7oz) ‹
Belgium's famous 'stinking cheese', a particularly strong type of
Herve which originated in Battice in the reign of the Emperor
Charles V (1519–58). Usually larger and ripened for longer
than the normal Herve, it has a darker, brownish-orange rind.
The name is derived from *remoud*, a Walloon word for the
exceptionally rich milk provided towards the end of the
lactation period. Nowadays mostly factory-made.

Royal Brabant
Small washed-rind cheese similar to Limburger.

Saint-Bernard   ⚄ ☾ 50% ⌔ 4kg (9lb) ‹
Similar to Dutch Gouda. Lightly salty with a tough black rind
and a creamy yellow smooth paste.

Trappistenkaas see *Fromage de Trappiste*

Vacheloo
Semi-hard cows' milk Saint-Paulin type: plain (yellow rind),
spiced (black rind) or with peppercorns (red rind).

BOLIVIA, BRAZIL see *Latin America*.

British Isles

ENGLAND

Geographically and climatically Britain is perfect for cheesemaking. Numerous breeds of sheep and cattle are raised on terrain that ranges from fertile water meadows to coarse scrub, yet even so, the range of cheese types is oddly limited. British cheeses are, at their best, truly excellent and unlike almost any others in the world. Sadly, they are virtually unknown, with one or two notable exceptions, outside Britain and the British themselves, with their inimitable capacity for underrating their own best efforts, often denigrate their own cheeses in favour of more exotic imports. It is true that the range of textures and tastes is less extensive than that of, say French or Italian cheeses, possibly because the British have been left alone for centuries to develop their own gastronomic style with a minimum of outside influences. The last great invasion of an alien taste and culture occurred in the 11th century when the Normans made their mark on every facet of British life, including cheesemaking. By the 16th century practically every county, if not every parish, had its own cheese (often referred to as 'white meat', which shows that the precise nutritional value of cheese was acknowledged even then). Most of these ancient cheeses are now extinct. Those that remain are almost exclusively cows' milk cheeses of the semi-hard or hard varieties and include one of the most popular cheeses in the world (Cheddar) and one of the most celebrated (Stilton).

There have been several disasters in British cheesemaking history which account, at least in part, for the comparative decline of British cheese. The first was the cattle epidemic of 1860 when thousands of cows were slaughtered. This led to a shortage of cheese and subsequently to massive imports of American factory-made Cheddar which paved the way for the industrialization of cheesemaking along American lines. This, combined with commercial pressures to meet burgeoning demand from the growing urban centres, meant that quantity superseded quality and the small farmer could no longer compete. Nevertheless, many small cheesemakers struggled on into the 20th century until World War II dealt another blow. Food rationing was introduced and with it stringent controls on food manufacture. Most milk was commandeered for the liquid market and so-called 'luxury' cheese varieties and those with minimal keeping qualities were banned. Before the war there were 1,500 farmhouse cheesemakers. In 1945 only 126.

Things however are by no means as bleak now as they were in the immediate postwar era. Thanks to an energetic campaign by the English Country Cheese Council and the Milk Marketing Board

the decline of authentic British cheeses made in the traditional way seems to have been reversed. The Farmhouse Cheesemaking Scheme, introduced in 1954, took over the marketing and grading of farmhouse cheese. The scheme covers Cheddar, Cheshire and Lancashire cheese. These farmhouse cheeses bear the Farmhouse English Cheese symbol (see page 23), which guarantees that they have been made on English farms in the traditional way and are of the highest quality. They are graded superfine, fine, graded or ungraded. Only the first two are sold as farmhouse cheese.

Farmhouse cheesemaking in Britain accounts at present for about ten per cent of total cheese production (the rest is made in creameries or cheese factories), but the signs are that interest in traditionally made cheese is steadily increasing. Throughout the country there are farms and small dairies busily re-creating traditional cheeses (apart from those covered by the official scheme), inventing new ones and simultaneously helping to establish a powerful rearguard action against the plastic-wrapped rindless blocks that crowd the supermarket counters.

Applewood

One of several recently invented cheeses that are rapidly gaining in popularity, although none is particularly original since they are mostly traditional cheeses flavoured with various herbs and spices. This one is Cheddar smoked over applewood and coated with paprika. There is another, virtually identical, known as Charnwood.

(On Stilton)
There are, of course, we know, those who prefer other cheeses . . . we wait with serene confidence for the day when they shall see the error of their ways. When, in due course, they do so, they can join the elect by all means, there is plenty of room at the end of the queue.
Edward & Lorna Bunyard THE EPICURE'S COMPANION

Blue Cheshire ★   48%   22kg (48lb)

A blue-veined cheese made in Shropshire and Cheshire. At one time Cheshires blued naturally but so rarely and unpredictably that it was more a matter of luck than judgement. This still happens occasionally and the resulting cheese is called Green Fade. Nowadays science has taken a hand and a degree of artifice is employed in the veining: *Penicillium roquefortii* is added to the milk before renneting. The cheese is pressed less than ordinary Cheshire and is aerated with steel needles during ripening. Only red farmhouse Cheshires are 'blued' and the maturation period is a little longer than usual—about three months. Blue Cheshire is still fairly hard to find and it is correspondingly expensive. Its flavour is exceedingly rich since the natural saltiness of mature Cheshire combines with the additional sharpness of the mould. According to Cheshiremen, Blue Cheshire should be eaten with plain chocolate biscuits. See *Cheshire*

Blue Shropshire

Dark orange cows' milk cheese with vigorous deep blue veining and an uneven crusty rind. Strong piquant flavour.

'Dairy Crest' indicates that this dairy operates under the auspices of the British Milk Marketing Board

Dairy Crest
Blue Stilton Cheese
J.M. Nuttall & Co Hartington Buxton Derbyshire

J.M. Nuttall is now the only dairy in England still making Blue Wensleydale

Blue Stilton ★   48% 2–8kg (4–18lb)

Velvety, close-textured unpressed cheese with a smooth, creamy white to pale ivory paste, grading to amber at the edges and marbled with a network of greenish-blue veins. The rind is dry, crusty, greyish brown and slightly wrinkled with white powdery patches. The flavour ranges from mild with a sharp edge when young, to rich and tangy when mature. Stilton, known everywhere as the 'King of English cheeses' is one of the few with any reputation in other countries. It already existed in 1727, when Daniel Defoe mentioned 'Stilton, a town famous for cheese'. In fact, Stilton was never made at Stilton, although it was sold there from the Bell Inn to coach travellers on the Great North Road. Its actual origins are somewhat hazy. We do know that the landlord of the Bell Inn was married in the early 18th century to one of the daughters of Elizabeth Scarbrow, housekeeper to Lady Beaumont at Quenby Hall near Leicester. Mrs Scarbrow was famous for her cheeses, which were known first as Lady Beaumont's cheese and later as Quenby cheese. A second daughter married Farmer Paulet of Wymondham and continued to make cheese according to her mother's recipe. This cheese was supplied to the Bell Inn and became known as Stilton. Whether it was the original Stilton, nobody knows.

Nowadays Stilton is made in 12 dairies scattered around Leicestershire, Nottinghamshire and Derbyshire and protected by a certificated trade mark. One of the dairies still uses unpasteurised milk, but otherwise milk is collected from neighbouring farms and pasteurized at the dairy. A culture of *Penicillium roquefortii* is added to the milk with the starter and rennet is added a short time later. After renneting the curds are cut by hand into small cubes and allowed to settle on the bottom of the vat. They may then either be ladled into draining troughs or run off together with the whey into coolers. In both cases they are left to drain until the following morning, when they are milled, salted and placed in plastic or stainless steel hoops for three days to a week. During this time each cheese is turned daily to drain further. Once removed from the hoops each cheese is rubbed down by hand to smooth out creases and seal the edges. The cheeses are then stored in precise conditions of temperature and humidity for an average of three to four months, when the characteristic crust will develop. During the first month the cheeses are turned every day and at eight weeks they are pierced with steel needles to promote veining.

The best Stilton (in the shops from September onwards) is made from summer milk and is distinguishable by a slightly yellower paste than usual. The age at which it should be eaten is largely a question of personal taste. Obviously as the cheese ages the mould spreads and the flavour deepens, but the rate varies from cheese to cheese. Personally I like to taste the cheese as well

21

as the mould and prefer a Stilton about four months old. When buying Stilton look for one where the veins are evenly distributed throughout the paste and where there is a good contrast between the creamy yellow paste and the blue streaks. Avoid a cheese where the paste is dry, cracked or brownish (except at the edges). Stilton is an excellent dessert cheese and is traditionally accompanied by port. At one time it was fashionable to pour the port into the middle of a cut whole cheese (producing what Ambrose Heath called 'a purplish kind of mash of cheese and wine of the most disgusting smell and appearance') and then scoop it out with a spoon. This practice is now universally frowned upon. See *White Stilton*

Blue Vinny
Does Blue Vinny actually exist any more? It certainly *has* existed for there are still people who claim to have eaten it in the past. It was made only in Dorset from partly skimmed cows' milk and was an extremely hard, white, blue-veined cheese. One of the many tall tales surrounding Blue Vinny (sometimes called Dorset Blue) insists that veining was encouraged by steeping old leather harnesses and even boots in the milk. Perhaps this explains its apparently sudden demise. Something labelled Blue Vinny can occasionally be found in cheese shops, but such a cheese is almost certainly second-grade Stilton.

Blue Wensleydale ★   48%   2.5kg (5½lb)
An exquisite close-textured blue-veined cheese. The paste is white with the barest hint of cream and has a delicate, almost honeyed flavour. It is made in the same way as Wensleydale except that *Penicillium roquefortii* is added to the milk. The cheese is pressed for only 24 hours before being transferred to the cheese store, where it is turned regularly, pierced to help the mould develop and matured for at least six weeks. It is, if anything, more temperamental than Stilton and more trouble to make. Perhaps because of this it is now made by only one dairy in the Dove valley, Derbyshire and is consequently not easy to find. See *Wensleydale*

Cambridge
One of the few traditional soft cheeses still occasionally available—a delectable mixture of plain and annatto-coloured curds made from raw or pasteurized cows' milk curdled with rennet. Naturally drained on straw mats, it is sold fresh or ripened for a few weeks. Sometimes known as York cheese.

Charnwood see *Applewood*

Cheddar ★   48%   5–27kg (11–59lb)
Golden yellow, close-textured cheese ranging in flavour from sweet and mild when young to mellow and nutty when mature. Cheddar is a much-maligned cheese, known irreverently to many as 'mousetrap'. It is very much a victim of its own success and is all too frequently treated with the contempt that almost inevitably accompanies such ubiquity.

Things were not always so: in Queen Elizabeth I's time one observer wrote of Cheddars being so prized that they were 'bespoke before they were made'. But the making of Cheddar, which began near the Somerset village of that name, has spread throughout the world, not only to ex-British colonies. Egypt, Japan and Czechoslovakia among many other countries produce Cheddar: it is the most widely made cheese in the world. Unfortunately the quality has suffered. Of the millions of people who eat Cheddar daily, only a few will have tasted the real farmhouse product, the 'excellent prodigious cheeses . . . of delicate taste' that William Camden enthused about. There are now only 26 farms left in the West Country of England still producing Cheddar by traditional methods. These farmhouse Cheddars rank among the finest cheeses in the world. The distinctive process is the 'cheddaring' (see Glossary), which takes place after the curds have been cut into tiny pea-sized pieces, scalded in the whey, pitched and cut into blocks. This slow, persistent draining of as much moisture as possible and the subsequent heavy pressing give the cheese its smooth, hard texture that, ideally, never crumbles when cut.

Cheddars are sold at various stages in their maturity. The 'mild' Cheddar marketed by the creameries is between three and five months old while 'mature' is over five and up to nine months or possibly more. Some good farmhouse cheese is kept longer—up to 18 months or even two years. Cheddar is a fine eating cheese and is also excellent for cooking, especially when good matured farmhouse Cheddar is used.

This label graces all farmhouse-made Cheddar, Cheshire and Lancashire. The latter two cheeses are always made from unpasteurized milk. Cheddars can be either. A reliable guarantee of good cheese

Cheshire ★   🐄 🌢 48% ▢ 4–22kg (9–48lb) ● ℂ

Moist, friable, slightly salty cheese, mild when young but acquiring a more pronounced tang with age. The paste is 'white' (pale yellow) or 'red' (annatto-dyed to a deep peach colour). Red Cheshire tends to be more popular in the Midlands and the South of England and White Cheshire in the North, but there is no difference in the flavour.

Cheshire is the oldest British cheese. It was mentioned in Domesday Book in 1086, but the evidence of folklore suggests that it is much older, going back, perhaps, even earlier than the Roman occupation. One story (told by Cheshiremen with more than a touch of pride) tells how the Romans hanged a cheesemaker at Chester Cross for refusing to divulge the recipe. The Romans were wasting their time: Cheshire can only be made from the milk of cattle grazed on the salty pastures of the Cheshire Plain, either in Shropshire or Cheshire. The Chester produced in France and many other European countries is related to English Cheshire in name only.

Most Cheshire nowadays is creamery-made, but there are still about 20 farms producing farmhouse cheeses. The cheese takes only about two to three hours to make. Evening and morning milk are mixed and after coagulation the curds are scalded in the whey for about 40 minutes. Then the whey is drained off very quickly while the cheesemaker cuts the curd and then tears it into small pieces. It is then salted, milled, put into moulds and pressed for between 24 and 48 hours. Some farmhouse Cheshires are still bandaged in the traditional way with cheese cloths dipped in lard. Others are dipped in wax. The cheeses are usually ripened for between four and eight weeks, but sometimes a particularly fine one will be selected for longer ripening, which may be anything up to 15 months.

Cheshire is a very even-tempered cheese. It is almost always good and often superb. Choose a farmhouse cheese if possible, even though Cheshire suffers less from factory methods than do most other cheeses. There are no hidden pitfalls in buying Cheshire: if it looks bright and fresh, buy it; if it is dry and cracked or sweating inside a vacuum pack, leave it alone. It is an excellent all-purpose cheese. Its flavour makes it especially delicious in omelettes and soufflés. See *Blue Cheshire*

Cheviot
Brand name for a blend of mild Cheddar with chopped chives.

Colwick
Recently revived soft fresh cow's milk cheese made to a traditional recipe. White, smooth and creamy with an agreeable, mildly sour flavour.

Cotherstone   48%   1–2kg (2–4lb)
Blue-veined cheese made from unpasteurized milk on two farms near Cotherstone, Yorkshire, between May and December. Once also known as Yorkshire Stilton, it is open-textured with a soft crust and a sharp flavour and is ripened for up to two months. Like Wensleydale and Swaledale, Cotherstone was introduced by monks who came over from Normandy with William the Conqueror. Mostly sold locally.

Cotswold
Double Gloucester flavoured with chopped onions and chives— a modern invention, though there is good historical precedent for flavouring cheese with herbs and, of course, the cheese and onion combination has long been a British favourite. In this cheese, the irresistible force of Double Gloucester meets the immovable tang of chives which are, in fact, quite overpowering. Not unpleasant but best taken in small doses.

Cottage Cheese
Cooked, skimmed cows' milk curds, drained, washed and coated with thin cream to produce a pure white, bland, low-fat granular cheese which is usually sold prepacked in tubs. It is eaten fresh with fruit or salad vegetables or used in cooking, such as for cheesecake. It can be an acceptable culinary substitute for Italian Ricotta.

Cream Cheese
Small unripened rennet-curd cows' milk cheeses made from single or double cream. Eaten fresh or used in cooking.

Curd Cheese
Acid-curd unripened cows' milk cheese available with low or medium fat content. Also known as lactic-curd cheese.

Derby   48%   4–14kg (9–31lb)
Mild, primrose yellow cheese with a close rather flaky texture. Neither a particularly interesting nor a popular cheese possibly because it is almost always sold far too young at between four and six weeks old. Ideally it should be ripened for around six months, but such mature Derbys are rare even in specialist shops. Derby cheese has the distinction of having been industrialized earlier than any other English cheeses, for the

first cheese factory opened near Derby in 1870. Farmhouse production has now ceased entirely. Traditionally, Derby is eaten with soft bread rolls and a mixture of sliced onions steeped overnight in sugar-sweetened vinegar. See *Sage Derby*

Double Gloucester ★ 🐄 🌙 48% ⊟ 4–14kg (9–31lb) 🌙
Bright orange, waxy cheese with a strong mellow flavour. Originally Gloucesters were coloured artificially (first with carrot juice or saffron and later with annatto) only for the London market, where buyers thought the magnificent colour indicated a richer, creamier cheese. The locals had no need to be deceived into buying it: they knew only too well how good it was. Most Double Gloucester is now creamery made and coloured although there are a few farms making both white and coloured versions. One farm still uses the unpasteurized milk of the original breed of Gloucester cattle and this is creamier even than Guernsey milk. Evening and morning milk are mixed before renneting; at one time they were skimmed and the cream added separately at a different temperature. The best Double Gloucester is that made from summer milk and aged for at least four months. See *Single Gloucester*

We may, indeed, divide cheeses into two groups, the romantic and the classic. They are easily distinguished. The romantics are apt to run over and become a little offensive when overripe. Classic cheeses do not; age may set them a little more firmly, but they never give way to it. Pungency and sting they have, but all within the limits of decency.
Edward & Lorna Bunyard THE EPICURE'S COMPANION

Eskdale
Rare soft Camembert-type unpressed cheese made from Jersey cows' milk on a single farm in Cleveland, Yorkshire.

Forest Cheese
Small farmhouse Double Gloucester, blued naturally, flavoured with cider vinegar and coated with chopped nuts.

Green Fade see *Blue Cheshire*

Herefordshire
Farmhouse cheese made between May and October from the unpasteurized milk of Jersey or Welsh Black cattle.

Huntsman
A modern 'invention' which is no more than a pointless marketing gimmick: layers of Double Gloucester and Stilton.

Ilchester
A brand name for several modern cheese concoctions including Cheddar with beer and garlic, Double Gloucester and cider, Stilton and port.

Lancashire ★ 🐄 🌙 48% ⊟ 4–18kg (9–40lb) 🍎 🌙
White, slightly salty, crumbly cheese with a rich, full-bodied flavour. Lancashire is underrated even in England, probably because most people know only the creamery type. An infinitely superior farmhouse version is made from unpasteurized milk on

five farms in the Preston area. Making Lancashire in the traditional way is a laborious and time-consuming process. The curd made on one day is added to the previous day's curd, which has already been drained, salted and partly pressed. Both curds are then milled, placed in moulds, pressed for 24 hours, bandaged, waxed and ripened for (at best) two months. Lancashire is the softest of the English pressed cheeses. It is an excellent melting cheese and is therefore ideal for cooking. Once known as Leigh Toaster because of its particular suitability for Welsh Rarebit. See *Sage Lancashire*

Leicester ★   🏠 ⟩ 48% ⊟ 4–22kg (9–48lb) 🍂 (

Sometimes unnecessarily called Red Leicester (there is no other kind), this is a hard-pressed grainy cheese with a faint lemony bite. The colour, ranging from bright russet-gold to tomato-red, makes the huge wheels the most visually striking of all British cheeses. It is quick-ripening and sold between ten and twelve weeks old. A farmhouse version is made on a single farm in Somerset and this is matured for a little longer. Avoid a cheese with slightly paler blotches on the cut surface of the paste. A good melting cheese.

Mollington
Rare soft cheese made from unpasteurized cows' milk.

Nutwood
Cheddar flavoured with dried fruit, hazel nuts and cider.

Rutland
Cheddar flavoured with beer, garlic and parsley.

Sage Derby
Derby with green marbling produced by soaking sage leaves in chlorophyll and adding the juice to the curds. This process produces a more subtle flavour than the chopped leaves used in Sage Lancashire. Spinach juice was once used. See *Derby*

Sage Lancashire
Farmhouse Lancashire with chopped sage added to the curds. The flavour of sage is overpowering for some tastes. Sage cheeses were traditionally made for festive occasions such as Christmas and harvest festivals. Sometimes the flat surfaces of the cheese were also decorated with whole sage leaves. See *Lancashire*

Sherwood
A new-fangled blend of Double Gloucester and sweet pickle. Needless to say it has nothing to do with Sherwood Forest, the Sheriff of Nottingham or Robin Hood.

Single Gloucester
White, open-textured cheese which is softer and milder than Double Gloucester but is also made from the milk of Gloucester cows on a single farm in Gloucestershire. The processing is conducted at a lower temperature and a lower acidity level than that of Double Gloucester. The curds are cut more finely and the cheese ripened for only about two months. Once known as 'hay' cheese because it was especially popular at harvest time.

Swaledale
A creamy coloured mild cheese made between May and December from Jersey cows' milk and ripened for one to three

months. It is produced on only one farm in the Yorkshire Dales and like Wensleydale and Cotherstone is a legacy of William I's monastic companions. It was also once a blue ewe's milk cheese.

Walton
An exotic mix of Cheddar, Stilton and chopped walnuts, moulded and coated with half walnuts. More than anything else it tastes, not surprisingly, of walnuts.

Wensleydale ★   ☼ ● 48% ▭ 4–6kg (9–13lb) 《
Until recently, Wensleydale meant the blue-veined cheese we now know as Blue Wensleydale. Now, however, the white, unveined version is much more common and is what you will get if you ask for Wensleydale. It is a lightly pressed, smooth-textured cheese with a subtle, milky flavour which is clean and refreshing. Generally eaten young, at about a month old. It is not a cheese that improves with age, though a prize specimen may be matured for a few months longer. Traditionally eaten with apple pie, gingerbread or fruitcake.

White Wensleydale is often unfairly compared with Blue on the grounds that it is not 'the real thing'. Yet nor is the Blue. The original Wensleydale was a ewes' milk, soft, blue-veined cheese which must have been somewhat similar to Roquefort. This and other cheeses, such as Swaledale, Cotherstone and Coverdale (now extinct) were introduced into England by monastic orders who settled in the Yorkshire Dales after the Norman Conquest in 1066. The Wensleydale recipe was the property of the Cistercian monks of Jervaulx Abbey but other monasteries also made cheeses, usually, it seems, from ewes' milk. Some time after the Dissolution of the Monasteries in the 16th century, Wensleydale and other cheeses began to be made from cows' milk and production moved first to farmhouses and then later to small dairies. See *Blue Wensleydale*

White Stilton   ☼ ● 48% ▭ 6.5kg (14lb) 《
Bland, close-textured white cheese made in the same way as Blue Stilton except that *Penicillium roquefortii* is not added to the milk and the cheese is sold at about eight weeks old. If left, a White Stilton will blue naturally and this produces a slightly milder flavour than the 'normal' blue. See *Blue Stilton*

Windsor Red
Another modern concoction of Cheddar and elderberry wine. The paste is yellow, marbled with crimson splodges.

IRELAND

The lush pastures of Ireland are ideal for raising herds of productive dairy cattle and the dairy industry is, in fact, flourishing. Cheese production has increased hundreds of times over since the beginning of this century, yet none of this cheese mountain is composed of indigenous Irish cheese types. Almost all cheese made in Ireland is an imitation of 'foreign' cheese and most of it is exported. There are Irish versions of Cheddar, Cheshire, Wensleydale, Caerphilly, Leicester and Double Gloucester as well as Brie, Camembert, Gouda, Edam, Gruyère, Pont l'Evêque and Edam. Even cheeses with Irish-sounding names turn out to be variously convincing doppelgangers: Blarney is a yellow, waxy cheese with a bright red rind and large holes, otherwise known as Irish Swiss; Killarney is a Cheddar, while Wexford is really

Cheshire. The originality and creativity of the Irish, not to say their nationalism, so evident in other areas of life, seem to have deserted them entirely in the matter of cheese.

SCOTLAND

Scotland has no great reputation for cheese. Its most important indigenous cheese, Dunlop, takes second place in terms of production and in Scottish affections to Cheddar (dyed with annatto for the Scottish market). Scotland also has the dubious distinction of being the first country to introduce rindless cheese (in 1955). At one time several locally made cheeses (now extinct) were popular, among them Island of Coll cheese and Blue Highland cheese (said by some to be 'finer than Stilton'); there was also a much-praised ewes' milk cheese known as Crying-kebbuck which was traditionally eaten to celebrate the birth of a new baby.

Caboc
Fresh, white, unpressed cows' milk cheese with a crunchy coating of oatmeal. Creamy but very bland in flavour.

Crowdie
Fresh, rather sour-tasting, unpressed cheese made from un-pasteurized skimmed cows' milk curdled with rennet, enriched with cream and eaten as soon as possible after making. Once called Cruddy (curdy) Butter, it is traditionally eaten on Scottish farms for breakfast. Goats' milk Crowdie was also made at one time. In the Highlands these cheeses were enriched with butter rather than cream and were sometimes matured for several months.

Cheese is milk that has grown up . . . the older it grows the more manly it becomes, and in the last stages of senility it almost requires a room to itself, like the jokes consecrated to the smoking room.
        Edward & Lorna Bunyard THE EPICURE'S COMPANION

Dunlop   ☼ ➤ 48% ☐ 27kg (59lb) ● ⊂
Often described as Scottish Cheddar, which it closely resembles except that it is lighter in colour and texture and lacks the characteristic Cheddar 'bite'. As with many famous cheeses, a woman is credited with its invention. In this case it was Barbara Gilmour, who is said to have brought the recipe from Ireland at the time of Charles II. Previously only skimmed-milk cheeses were known in Scotland. The name derives from the village in Ayrshire where it was first made. It was also the name of the Ayrshire cows that originally provided the milk and, by a happy coincidence, the name of Barbara Gilmour's subsequent husband. Dunlop is now entirely creamery-made, although not in Dunlop itself.

Gigha
A hard orange cows' milk cheese from the Isle of Gigha, Argyll.

Orkney
Small, lightly pressed cows' milk cheeses from the remote islands off the north-east coast of Scotland. Available white,

coloured (orange with annatto) or smoked. Originally made from skimmed milk and sometimes matured in a barrel of oatmeal. Islay cheeses are very similar.

WALES

There are several tantalizing historical references to Welsh cheeses. At one time there was a spring-made Newport cheese—thick, creamy and square-moulded; Glamorgan cheese was made from the milk of a special breed of white cattle; a mixed cows' and goats' milk cheese, made in North Wales, once competed with Cheshire and, in some tortuous fashion, led to the custom of dyeing Cheshire red. The only traditional cheese of Welsh origin remaining is Caerphilly and even this is no longer made in Wales. Caerphilly is a comparative newcomer, but the Welsh passion for cheese—especially toasted—has been noted for centuries. The Welsh toast cheese in several ways: by melting the cheese in a pan with beer and seasoning, spreading it on bread and finishing it under the grill (Welsh Rarebit), or covering a slice of toast with cheese and grilling it, or baking it with an egg on top.

Caerphilly ★   48% 3–4kg (7–9lb)

Moist, crumbly, lemon yellow cheese with a salty, slightly sour buttermilk flavour, Caerphilly dates back only to the early 1800s. It was originally made not only in Caerphilly itself but also in dairy farms throughout the Vale of Glamorgan and in Gwent west of the River Usk, from the milk of Hereford cattle. For years it was known in Wales simply as 'new cheese' (a reference to its quick-ripening properties rather than its recent origins) and most of it was consumed locally both because relatively little was made and also because it did not travel well. Two batches were made daily, one from morning milk and one from evening milk, throughout the summer months. They were ready for sale within a week to ten days. This factor made them a tempting proposition for the Cheddar-makers on the other side of the Bristol Channel. Caerphilly could provide a quick turnover during the long months of waiting for Cheddars to mature and by the beginning of this century it was being made in large quantities in Somerset. In World War II the making of Caerphilly was banned completely and Welsh cheesemakers, without Cheddar to fall back on, never recovered from this blow. Nowadays Caerphilly is made entirely in England.

There are one or two farms in Somerset still making Caerphilly in the old way from unpasteurized milk. The cheese is rapidly drained and lightly pressed. Its rind is formed by soaking the cheese in brine for 24 hours after pressing and then whitened with rice flour. Farmhouse Caerphilly is best eaten a few days after making. The creamery version is matured for up to two weeks. Caerphilly is so mild and digestible that it can happily be eaten in large quantities. The Welsh crumble it on a slice of bread, add a few drops of vinegar and, of course, toast it.

Llangoffan

A rare cheese made from unpasteurized Jersey cows' milk, rich, soft and creamy with a golden yellow crust.

BULGARIA, CZECHOSLOVAKIA see *Eastern Europe*. CANADA see *North America and Canada*. CYPRUS see *Greece and Cyprus*. CHILE, COLOMBIA, COSTA RICA, CUBA see *Latin America*. DENMARK see *Scandinavia*.

Eastern Europe

Eastern Europe has been the battleground between Europe and Asia for centuries and political boundaries have been drawn and redrawn countless times. It is surprising, in these circumstances, to find that vigorous, identifiable, national gastronomic traditions have been able to develop and endure. Up to World War II, agriculture was the most important economic activity. Since then, however, things have changed, partly because of devastation caused by the war (Poland, for example, lost over half her cattle) and partly because postwar recovery emphasized industrial rather than agricultural development. Recent efforts to redress this balance have, in the case of cheesemaking, led to a concentration on mass market rather than traditional products. Large-scale collectivization has meant that small farms, except in remote mountain areas, have all but disappeared. Virtually all cheese is now made from pasteurized milk. Cheddar, Tilsit, Gouda, Emmental and many other popular European cheese types are mass-produced. In the north, traditional cheeses are generally related to German types such as Quark and the Handkäse varieties. There are also some interesting smoked cheeses not found elsewhere. In the south the Mediterranean influence is strong (a legacy of the Roman and Turkish occupations). Descendants of Caciocavallo and white brined ewes' milk cheeses are prevalent and some buffalo milk cheeses can still be found.

Balaton (Hungary)　　　🏺 🐄 45% 🧀 9–12kg (20–26lb) 🌙
Firm, hard-pressed, golden cheese with irregular holes and a thin rather greasy rind. The flavour is mildly acidulous. Ripened for five to six weeks. Named after Lake Balaton.

Balkanski Kâskaval (Балкански Кашкавал) (Bulgaria)
see *Kashkaval*

Bijeni Sir (Yugoslavia)　　　　　　🐄 35% 🧀 🅳
Sharp white cheese made from cows' or ewes' milk and ripened in brined whey. From Macedonia. Factory- and farm-made.

Brynza (Брынза) (Bulgaria)　　　　🐑 🐐 45% 🅱 🅱
Brînză (Romania), **Bryndza** (Hungary, Czechoslovakia, Poland)
Salty white brined cheese made in many parts of eastern Europe, particularly in the Carpathian mountains, usually from ewes' milk but occasionally from cows' or goats' milk. Available in several versions ranging from soft and spreadable to firm and crumbly. Sometimes also smoked. It is made in factories from partially ripened curds supplied by mountain shepherds. The curds are scraped of any rind, broken up, salted, milled and remoulded in blocks or packed into wooden barrels with yet more salt. Eaten raw, often cubed in salads or with olives, pickled vegetables and strong rye bread. It also features in a great many local dishes and can be used as a base for Liptauer. See *Liptói*.

Brînză de Burduf (Romania)　　　　🐑 🐐 45% 🌙
Strong, pungent, spreadable cheese ripened in an animal skin bag (a *burduf*). Has a yellow paste and a grey rind spotted with mould. Traditionally eaten at the end of Lent.

Dalia (Romania)
  Kashkaval made with cows' milk.

Dobrogea (Romania)
  Type of Kashkaval made with ewes' milk.

Feta(Фета)(Bulgaria, Yugoslavia)
  Originally a Greek cheese but also made for centuries in other
  Balkan countries, particularly Bulgaria. Exceptionally good
  Bulgarian ewes' milk Feta is occasionally exported to the West.
  If you find any, it is well worth trying. It is superb—creamier
  and more delicate than the more commonly available cows'
  milk types. See *Greece (Feta)*

Gomolya (Hungary), **Homolky, Hrudka** (Czechoslovakia)
  White ewes' milk cheese made on mountain farms. Eaten
  partially ripened or sold to factories for making Bryndza.
  Sometimes used as a base for Liptauer. See *Liptói*

Gruševina see *Urdă*

Hajdú (Hungary)
  Kashkaval made from cows' milk.

Homolky, Hrudka see *Gomolya*

Kashkaval (Кашкавал)   45%   ☐ 6–9kg (13–20lb) ● ℭ
  Made throughout the Balkan lands since Roman times and
  based on Italian Caciocavallo. The best cheeses are made from
  ewes' milk, although mixed milk and sometimes only cows' milk
  types are found. Like Caciocavallo the processing involves a
  kneading stage where the curds are immersed in hot water to
  make them malleable before being finally moulded, brined and
  aged for about two months. The mature cheeses range from
  almost white to golden yellow depending on the milk and are
  generally rather hard and crumbly in consistency. The flavour
  is mild and faintly salty to strong and nutty according to age.
  Kashkaval is the Cheddar of the Balkans, eaten as a table cheese
  and also used in cooking. Often it is cubed and fried. Old hard
  cheeses are used for grating. One of the best types is the
  Bulgarian Balkanski Kâskaval.

Kefalotir (Yugoslavia)
                  🐄 ➤ 45–50% ☐ 9–10kg (20–22lb) ● ℭ
  Hard Macedonian grating cheese with a smooth shiny rind, full
  flavour and pungent aroma. See *Greece (Kefalotiri)*

Lajta (Hungary)   ⚱ ➤ 52% ◻ 1kg (2lb) ℭ
  Piquant pale yellow cheese with numerous elliptical holes and a
  deep orange, moist, washed rind. Ripened for four weeks.

Liptói (Hungary), **Liptovská Bryndza** (Slovakia)
                              🐄 ◗ 50% ℭ
  Liptov in the Tatra mountains was reputedly the place where
  Bryndza was first made and its name is still used to denote
  particularly fine, white, creamy, soft ewes' milk cheeses made
  from whole unpasteurized milk. Such cheeses were the
  traditional base for a spread that is now widely known as
  Liptauer. The soft curd cheese is mixed with ingredients such
  as paprika, caraway seeds, onions or mustard or sometimes with
  anchovies and capers.

31

Mandur, Manur (Yugoslavia)　🥩　◗ 40% ○ 3kg (7lb) 🍐 €
Dry grating cheese made from the whey by-product of
Kashkaval and Kefalotir mixed with milk or buttermilk.

Moravský Bochnik　🏺 ◗ 45% ⊖ 13kg (28lb) 🍐 €
(Czechoslovakia)
Pressed cooked cheese with holes, modelled on Emmental.

Nasal (Romania)
Low-fat washed-rind cheese made from cows', ewes' or water
buffalo milk in the hills near Cluj.

Niva (Czechoslovakia)　🏺 🐌 50% ⊡ 2kg (4lb) €
Crumbly piquant blue-vein cheese made from pasteurized
milk. Ripened for two to three months and wrapped in foil.

Njeguški Sir (Yugoslavia)
Hard ewes' milk grating cheese from Montenegro.

Olomoucký Sýr (Czechoslovakia)
The prototype of Austrian Olmützer Quargel from Olomouc in
Moravia. Partially ripened lactic curd cheese (*quarg*) is drained,
pressed, milled and moulded into various shapes (usually small
discs or rolls). It is then further ripened in conditions designed to
produce various bacterial growths on the surface of the cheese.
The result is a curious translucent rubbery substance with a
very odd uncheese-like flavour and a pervasive smell.

Oštěpek, Oštiepok (Czechoslovakia), **Oszczpek** (Poland)
Spun-curd ovoid cheeses pressed in carved wooden moulds that
produce decorative impressions on the surface of the cheese.
After spending a day or so in brine the cheeses are smoked for up
to six days and vary in colour from warm golden to dark
chocolate brown depending on the length of smoking. Similar
cheeses shaped like hams and salamis are also made.

Óvár, Ovari (Hungary)　🏺 ◗ 45% ⊡ 3–4kg (7–9lb) €
A pressed Tilsit-type made from pasteurized milk.

Parenyica (Czechoslovakia, Hungary)
Sometimes called 'ribbon cheese', long strips of spun-curd
cheese rolled up and lightly smoked. Traditionally made with
ewes' milk. Now also factory-made from cows' milk.

Peneteleu (Romania)
Kashkaval made from ewes' milk.

Pivny Sýr (Czechoslovakia)　🏺 🐌 47% ⊂⊃ 1·8kg (4lb) €
Salty 'beer cheese' similar to West German Weisslacker. Straw-
coloured with a smeary yellow rind and strong sharp flavour.
Ripened for four to six months. Foil-wrapped.

Planinski Sir (Yugoslavia)　　14–18kg (30–40lb) 🍐 €
Dry Serbian 'mountain cheese' from Kosovo made in summer
and stored in brine for winter consumption.

Podhalanski (Poland)　🐌 ▱ 500g (18oz) €
Lightly smoked cheese made from ewes' and cows' milk.

Sirene (Сирене)(Bulgaria) ◗ 45% 500g–1kg (18oz–2lb) 🍐 €
The most popular and widely produced Bulgarian cheese.

Basically similar to Brinza, this white brined cheese is made either from ewes' or cows' milk. Crumbly, sharp and salty although the cows' milk type is milder.

Skuta see *Urda*

Somborski Sir (Yugoslavia)
From Sombor, Vojvodina. Soft, slightly bitter cheese made with ewes' milk or mixed ewes' and cows' milk diluted with a proportion of water. It has a strong-flavoured yellowish paste with medium holes and a thin rind. Ripened for three weeks stacked in wooden vessels during which time gases produced in the cheese expand causing it to rise like yeast dough.

Švapski Sir see *Urda*

Teasajt (Hungary)   45%   500g (18oz)
'Tea cheese', recently invented. It has a creamy yellow paste with small round holes and a smeary rind. Rather sour. Ripened for two weeks.

Telemea (Romania)
White brined cheese similar to Feta. Made from ewes' or cows' milk, or from cows' milk mixed with buffalo milk.

Teleorman (Romania)
Kashkaval made from mixed cows' and ewes' milk.

Travnički Sir (Yugoslavia)
From the town of Travnik, Bosnia. Made from ewes' or mixed ewes' and cows' milk. It has a softish white paste scattered with holes. The flavour is sour and salty.

Tvaroh (Slovakia), **Twaróg** (Poland)
White compact fresh curd cheese made of cows' or ewes' milk. In Czechoslovakia it is available in two forms: Mekky is soft and crumbly, eaten both as a spread and in salads and is also used to make cheesecake (*tvarohový koláč*); Tvrdy is the cheese ripened until it is dry and hard, when it is used for grating. It is one of the main ingredients in the pastry for fruit dumplings. In Poland the aged type (*zgliwiaty ser*) is often fried with eggs.

Urdâ (Romania), **Urda** (Czechoslovakia, Yugoslavia)
Fresh, unsalted, soft whey cheese. Eaten with herbs as a spread or used in cooking. Similar to Italian Ricotta. Also called Švapski Sir, Gruševina.

Warszawski (Poland)
Ewes' milk cheese similar to Kashkaval.

Zlato (Czechoslovakia)   50%   1·5kg (3lb)
Sweetish cheese with a golden paste and a dry orange rind.

Key words	
Brînză (Romania) cheese	**Sir** (Yugoslavia)
Sajt (Hungary)	**Sirene (Сирене)** (Bulgaria)
Ser (Poland)	**Sýr** (Czechoslovakia)

EGYPT see *Middle East*. EL SALVADOR see *Latin America*. FINLAND see *Scandinavia*.

France

Boulogn

PAYS

Neufchâtel-B

Forges-les-Eaux

Le Havre

Pont-l'Evêqu

PAYS D'AUGE

CALVADOS

NORMANDY • Vimoutiers

• Camembert

Brest

• Rennes • Entrammes

BRITTANY

Laval

MAYENNE

MAINE-ET-LOIRE

Orle

ANJOU

Selles-sur-Ch

• Nantes

Loire

Arnon

TOURAINE Valer

VENDEE

Poulign

St. Pier

POITOU

• Poitiers

• Couhé-Verac

• La Mothe

Saint-Héray

AUNIS

OLERO

BAY OF

BISCAY

CORSICA

• Lime

Bordeaux

Dordogne

DORDOGNE

Garonne

AQUITAINE

PERIGORD

QUERC

GASCONY

Toulouse

BEARN

Oloron-Sainte-Marie

ARIÈGE

BASQUE

COUNTRY

PYRENEES

Foix

SPAIN

ANDORRA

▢ 500m

▢ 200m

French cheese is undoubtedly the best in the world.
Although there are individual cheeses from other countries
which may be as good as, or even better than, the best of
French cheeses, no country offers a range of cheeses that for
inventiveness, consistently high quality, authenticity and
sheer variety of flavour and texture, comes anywhere near
the French selection. French cheeses encompass virtually all
the cheese types produced in other countries and hundreds

MEDITERRANEAN SEA

more besides. A number of foreign cheeses—Gouda, Edam, Feta and Passé l'An (Parmesan)—are made in France but, on the whole, the French prefer to concentrate on maintaining the quality, variety and authenticity of their own indigenous cheeses and there is a considerable body of legislation directed towards these ends. Local cheesemaking traditions are jealously guarded. Cheesemakers have endeavoured, often successfully, to protect their products by legal means for hundreds of years. This is perhaps one reason why the subtle differences between French local cheeses have not been overwhelmed by the tide of industrialized uniformity which has swept aside so many traditional cheeses in other countries.

The efforts of the cheesemakers have also been encouraged by the enviable reputation that French cheeses have always enjoyed both at home and abroad—ever since the Romans returned home from France with memories of the excellence of Roquefort and Cantal. The taste for cheese was certainly encouraged by their presence and continued to grow long after they had left. Charlemagne championed the cause of many great cheeses of the day and tales of his 'discoveries' are legion. During the Middle Ages cheesemaking moved into the monasteries, oases of peace in turbulent times, where so many facets of civilized life were preserved for posterity. Such places nurtured the huge family of French monastic cheeses—Maroilles, Munster, Pont l'Evêque and all the Trappist cheeses are their legacies.

During the Renaissance fresh cheeses became particularly fashionable, especially among the rich. (Aged, hard, strong cheeses were thought to be food only for workers and peasants.) Jonchées and Caillebottes were essential ingredients of the fabulous desserts and pastries that were the crowning glories of sumptuous banquets. Fresh cheeses such as these are still found in France today in greater variety than anywhere else. Equally there are more ewes' milk cheeses, more blue cheeses and, in particular, more goats' milk cheeses than anywhere else in the world.

The extraordinary richness of French cheesemaking is rooted in geographical diversity and maintained by that lively interest in the good things of life that is the mark of French culture generally. One might think that with so many cheeses the French would see neither sense nor profit in inventing more and yet there are no signs that their creativity is flagging. New cheeses appear almost every day. Some (like so many recently invented cheeses) are mere affectations, novelties designed to titillate the eye or the imagination rather than the palate, but many are really excellent and well worth investigating. I have included a selection of the latter in the listing alongside the classic cheeses which they complement but by no means replace. Also included are many cheeses that never leave France or even, in some cases, the village where they are made. Dedicated cheesehounds will seek them out. Others may indulge in a little harmless fantasizing.

Abondance   🗇 ➌ 40% ⊟ 5–20kg (11–44lb) ◖
Firm smooth pressed farmhouse cheese made in Savoie from partly skimmed milk of the Abondance breed of cattle. It has a dry, grey rind and a mild, fruity flavour and is ripened for up to three months. Also called Tomme d'Abondance. Quite a different cheese may be sold either under the same name or as Vacherin d'Abondance. This small washed-rind cheese is also made in Savoie from milk of the same breed and encircled by a strip of spruce bark.

Aisy Cendré   🗇 ➋ 45% ⊟ 600–800g (21–28oz) ◖
Strong-smelling, tangy, washed-rind cheese from Montbard in Burgundy. Ripened for two months and stored in the ashes of

vine stems. Named after a village in Epoisses. Also called Cendré d'Aisy. See *Cendré*

Aligot see *Tomme Fraîche*
Altier see *Pelardon*

Amou   🥩 🍶 45% 🧀 4–5kg (9–11lb) 🅾️

Pressed uncooked farmhouse cheese made in Gascony on the edge of Les Landes. It has a thin, oiled, golden rind and a smooth firm paste with a mild, slightly tangy flavour. Ripened for a minimum of two months, when the cheese is faintly reminiscent of Saint-Paulin, and up to six months. The older, harder cheeses are grated and used in regional dishes.

Anduze see *Pelardon*

Ardi-Gasna   🥩 🍶 45% 🧀 4–5kg (9–11lb) 🌑 🅾️

Made on mountain farms in the Basque country. A firm, smooth, pressed cheese with a pronounced sheepy aroma matched by a full mellow flavour. Best eaten after three months. Also called Arnéguy, Esterençuby.

Asco

Small round Corsican cheese made from ewes' milk or a mixture of ewes' and goats' milk. Eaten from early spring to late autumn. Similar to Niolo.

Aunis   🍶 45% 250–300g (9–10oz) 🅾️

An increasingly rare soft Poitevin cheese made of cows', ewes' or goats' milk. Triangular in shape, it has a greyish, powdery rind.

Autun

Burgundian soft cheese made entirely from goats' milk or from a mixture of goats' and cows'. The fat content varies with the type of milk used, but should be at least 35 per cent.

Baguette   🏛️ 🍶 45% 🍥 500g (18oz) 🥖

Recently invented cheese from Laon. A type of Maroilles with a rich creamy yellow paste, a soft brown washed rind and the typical aroma of this family of cheeses. Factory-made and ripened in humid conditions for three or four months. Best from summer to the end of the year. Usually sold boxed. A smaller, rather milder version is known as Demi-Baguette. Also called Baguette Laonnaise, Baguette de Thierache.

Banon ★   🍶 45% 🧀 100–200g (3½–7oz) 🐐

Delicious small cheese from Provence. The authentic farmhouse version is made either from goats' or ewes' milk, depending on the time of year. The dairy variety is usually a cows' milk cheese with a mild, slightly sour flavour, or a *michèvre*. Instantly recognizable by its chestnut leaf wrapping and raffia ties. The leaves are previously soaked in eau-de-vie and grape marc and the parcels are left to ferment in terracotta jars for anything from two weeks to two months. The cows' milk types can be eaten all year round; the ewes' and goats' are best in spring and summer, and in summer and autumn respectively. Banon au Pèbre d'Aï (also known as Poivre d'Ane or La Sarriette) is a similar cheese, but after draining it is rolled in sprigs of savory (*pèbre d'aï* in Provençal dialect). Sold in boxes lined with savory (*pèbre d'aï* in Provençal dialect). Banon can also be found with various flavourings.

Barberey   🏠 🌙 30% 🧀 250g (9oz) 🅓
Simple rustic cheese with a rather mellow flavour ripened in wood ash, made from partly skimmed milk in small dairies around Troyes. Also called Fromage de Troyes, Troyen Cendré.

Beaufort ★   🏠 🌙 50% 🧀 20–60kg (44–132lb) 🌰 🐄
'The prince of Gruyères' according to Brillat-Savarin—a hard-pressed cooked cheese, moulded into huge golden cartwheels and ripened for about six months in cool caves. It has been made in the high mountains of Beaufort in Savoie for centuries and probably dates back to Roman times. Higher in fat than the other Gruyères, Comté and Emmental, it has a marvellously fruity aroma, rich flavour and a smooth, creamy, buttery paste with very few, if any, holes or cracks. The best is Beaufort de Montagne or Beaufort Haute Montagne, descriptions legally restricted to cheeses made from summer milk in Beaufort, Haute Tarentaise and the Col de la Madeleine-en-Maurienne and at their best between September and May. There is also a Beaufort Laitier or Beaufort d'Hiver, which is made in small dairies during the winter. Protected by an *appellation d'origine*. See *Gruyère*

Beauges see *Vacherin des Beauges*

Beaumont   🏠 🌙 50% 🧀 1–5kg (3lb) 🐄
Mild, creamy, factory-made cheese with a smooth, pliant, pinkish-brown rind, similar in many ways to Reblochon. Invented in 1881 in Beaumont, Haute-Savoie. An unpasteurized version is also available on a small scale.

Belle Bressane   🏠 🌙 50% 2kg (4lb) 🐄
Modern, soft, blue-veined cheese shaped like a ring and made from pasteurized milk. Fairly mild, rich and creamy.

Belval   🏠 🌙 40% 🧀 2kg (4lb) 🅓
Mild, white, pressed cheese with a shiny golden rind made at the Abbey of Belval in Picardy. Also known as Abbaye de Belval, Trappiste de Belval.

Bergues   🏠 🌙 20% 🧀 2kg (4lb) 🌰 🅓
Made in Flanders, near Dunkirk, from skimmed or partly skimmed milk. A tangy, strong-smelling cheese that is washed with beer and brine during its three-week ripening period. Once a 'workers' cheese', popular before the war because of its low price, it is now increasingly rare. Sometimes aged up to two months, and used for grating.

Bethmale   🏠 🌙 45% 🧀 5–7kg (11–15lb) 🌰 🐐
Firm, spicy cheese made in the foothills of the Pyrenees in summer and in lowland villages around Foix in winter. Aged for about three months, it is best in spring and summer. Sometimes ewes' milk may be used, either alone or mixed with cows'. Local variations include Aulus, Ercé, Oust, Saint-Lizier.

Béthune
Known affectionately as 'old stinker' (*vieux puant*), a Fromage Fort made from Maroilles curds flavoured with pepper and herbs and sealed in jars for several months to ferment. Said to have been invented by miners who, no doubt wisely, wash it down with a glass of gin.

Bibbelskäse
  Mild, fresh cows' milk cheese from Alsace, flavoured with horseradish and herbs.

Billy
  Small goats' milk cheese made near Selles-sur-Cher. Wrapped in plane leaves to ripen and packed in stoneware crocks.

Bleu
  Generic term for blue-veined cows' milk cheese. The Juras and the Massif Central are the best areas for blue cheeses. Bleu can also describe a cheese with a blue-tinged natural rind such as Olivet Bleu or, occasionally, a Cendré.

Bleu d'Auvergne ★ 🏵 ⊗ 45% ☐ 2.5–4.5kg (5½–10lb) **ზ**
  From the Massif Central, particularly the *départements* of Cantal and Puy-de-Dôme and the mountains of Cantal and Aurillac. Since each Bleu takes very much less milk to make than Cantal—the other great cheese of the area—it was more suited to the small farmer. The cheeses used to be brought down the mountain twice a week on donkeys or mules and sold to co-operative *affineurs* for ripening. The best Bleu d'Auvergne is still made on mountain farms by traditional methods, but a great deal is now also made in commercial dairies from pasteurized milk. It is a lightly piquant creamy cheese which has a very pale paste with sharply defined dark blue veining throughout the body of the cheese. The mould, *Penicillium glaucum*, is added either at the renneting stage or sprinkled in powder form on to the moulded curds. The cheese is ripened in cool cellars for an initial period of two months, when it is regularly turned and pierced with steel needles to distribute the mould. Then it is wrapped in foil to mature slowly for another month or so. The label should show that it is a legally protected cheese.

Bleu de Bresse 🏵 ⊗ 50% ☐ **ზ**
  Mildly spicy blue-veined cheese with a rather undignified history. It is a variation on an imitation. Restrictions on the import of Gorgonzola during World War II led to the development of a French imitation known as Saingorlon. Bleu de Bresse, invented in 1950, is a smaller, more easily marketable version of the same cheese. It comes in three sizes, *mini*, *moyen* and *maxi* —weighing between 100 and 500g (3½–18oz). A factory-made product using pasteurized milk.

Beware of young women who love neither wine nor truffles nor cheese nor music.
  Colette PAYSAGES ET PORTRAITS

Bleu des Causses 🏵 ⊗ 45% ⊜ 2.5kg (5½lb) **ზ**
  Similar to Bleu d'Auvergne but saltier. From Rouergue in the midst of the stark limestone country known as Les Causses which provides the natural caves used for ripening the cheeses. The name is legally protected.

Bleu de Corse 🏵 ⊗ 45% ☐ 2kg (4lb) **D**
  Most of the ewes' milk cheese made in Corsica is sent 'white' to the Roquefort caves to be blued. Bleu de Corse is the name for cheese that is ripened in Corsica itself. Since most people prefer Roquefort this cheese is fast dying out.

Bleu de Gex ⚗ 🐄 45% ▢ 6–8kg (13–18lb) 🐄

A naturally blued cheese from Franche Comté, first made about 100 years ago. The rind is powdery dry and rather crusty with yellowish or reddish tinges. The paste is smooth white, marbled with deep blue. Lightly pressed, it has a full flavour with a mildly sharp edge. The best is made in Saint Germain-de-Joux in summer and autumn. Once made on mountain farms, now in small co-operative dairies.

Bleu du Haut-Jura

The legal term for the much sought-after Bleu de Gex and Bleu de Septmoncel. Protected by an *appellation d'origine*.

Bleu de Laqueuille ⚗ 🐄 45% ▢ 2–3kg (4–7lb) 🐄

A lightly piquant blue from the Auvergne, invented in 1850. Factory-made and milder than Bleu d'Auvergne, it is ripened for about three months at relatively high temperatures.

Bleu du Quercy ⚗ 🐄 45% ▢ 2kg (4lb) 🐄

From Aquitaine, a blue cheese similar to Bleu d'Auvergne.

Bleu de Sassenage ⚗ 🐄 45% ▢ 5–6kg (11–13lb) 🐄

Lightly pressed blue cheese similar to Bleu de Gex in the area of Villard-de-Lans and Vallonnais in the province of Dauphiné. Uses partly skimmed milk and is ripened for about three months. Once made from cows', goats' or ewes' milk or a mixture of any two, but now exclusively from cows' milk.

Bleu de Septmoncel ⚗ 🐄 45% ▢ 5–6kg (11–13lb) 🐄

Has a slightly smoother rind but otherwise virtually identical to Bleu de Gex. See *Bleu du Haut-Jura*

Bleu de Thiézac ⚗ 🐄 45% ▢ 2–3kg (4–7lb) 🐄

A variation of Bleu d'Auvergne produced exclusively on mountain farms and much prized, especially from Thiézac itself.

Bonbel

Brand name for a factory-made Saint-Paulin. Baby Bel is a small French-made Edam from the same company, Bel.

Bondail, Bondard, Bondart see *Bondon*

Bondaroy au Foin ⚗ 🐄 40% ▢ 250g (9oz) 🐄

Small soft tangy cheese with a smooth, greyish rind covered with wisps of hay. Ripened in hay for about five weeks, hence the name (*foin*, hay). Also called Pithiviers au Foin.

Bondon ⚗ 🐄 50% ▢ 🐄

Originally a farmhouse cheese produced almost entirely for domestic consumption but now increasingly made in small dairies and factories on a commercial basis. It is a fresh or barely ripened soft cheese, with a light covering of white rind flora and comes from the Pays de Bray in Normandy, noted for its cider. The name Bondon reflects the shape of the cheese, which is similar to the *bonde* or bung of a cider barrel. Also called Bonde, Bondard, Bondart or, when flavoured with garlic, Bondail. There are several sizes and the ripening period varies from a few days for small cheeses (Bondons) to a few weeks for the largest ones (Bondards). Some very large ones were at one time ripened for several months and eaten on festive occasions by which time they were very piquant and the white rind had darkened to a brownish red. The name is also used for other similar cheeses moulded in the same shape, such as Bondon Neufchâtel. Cheeses like this have been made for at least 1,000 years.

Bossons Macérés 🦷 🍷 45% 🅓
A ferocious cheese from Provence made by steeping small goats' milk cheeses in a mixture of olive oil, herbs and white wine or eau-de-vie in a jar for several months. According to one writer it is *'parfaitement abominable et bon seulement pour les snobs'*.

Bougon 🦷 🍷 45% ⊟ 250g (9oz) 🅑
Factory-made Poitevin cheese with a pale, creamy paste and white rind flora. Pleasantly mild goaty flavour.

Bouille, La 🖒 🍷 60% ⊟ 200g (7oz) 🅑
Full-flavoured double-cream cheese from Normandy. Ripened for between two and three months. Covered with a thin downy white mould tinged with pink. Fairly strong fruity smell.

Boulette d'Avesnes 🖒 🍷 45% 160g (5oz) 🅑
There are two versions of this cheese. The authentic farmhouse type is made by heating buttermilk and draining and seasoning the resultant solids with herbs and spices. This mixture is then kneaded to a smooth paste, hand-moulded into small cones and ripened for at least three months in a humid environment, during which time the cheeses are regularly washed, usually with beer. The commercial type is ripened in the same way but uses unripened Maroilles curds rather than buttermilk solids as a base. Both cheeses are very tangy and strong-smelling with bright red rinds, which are natural in the case of farmhouse cheeses but often tinted in factory products. From Flanders.

Boulette de Cambrai 🖒 🍷 45% ○ 250g (9oz) 🅓
Fresh hand-moulded cheese, exclusively farmhouse-made, using skimmed or whole milk curds flavoured with salt, pepper, parsley, tarragon and sometimes chives. From Flanders.

Boursault 🖒 🍷 75% ⊟ 200g (7oz) 🅑
Small factory-made, triple-cream cheese, using pasteurized milk. Very rich and creamy with a soft, bloomy rind tinged with pink. Mildly aromatic and just mellow in flavour. Avoid it if at all red or runny. Named after its inventor and made in Normandy and the Île de France. A herb-flavoured version is also available. Sometimes called Lucullus.

Boursin 🖒 🍷 70% 🗋 🅐
Small, factory-made, triple-cream cheese using pasteurized milk. Available plain or flavoured with garlic and herbs, or crushed peppercorns. Should be eaten fresh.

Bouton-de-Culotte
Literally 'trouser button'. A tiny goats' milk cheese from Burgundy, dried and stored for winter use. Extra sharp with a dark greyish-brown rind, often grated or used in Fromage Fort. Also called Chevreton de Mâcon.

Bresse Bleu see *Bleu de Bresse*

Bricquebec
Saint-Paulin type made in Normandy at the abbey of the same name and sold under the brand name Providence.

Brie ★   🌼 ᠍🐄 40–50%   ᠍🧀 1–3kg (2–7lb)   🅐

After Camembert, the most famous and most imitated of all
French cheeses. It is, in fact, a much older cheese than
Camembert and can be documented by name at least as far
back as the 13th century. It boasts a string of illustrious admirers
including, it seems, virtually all the kings and queens of France.
Even Louis XVI, before his execution, asked for '*du vin rouge et du
Brie*'. Its supremacy was finally confirmed at the Congress of
Vienna in 1814. A cheese contest, organized by Talleyrand to
relieve the boredom of the assembled throng of diplomats and
princes, resulted in the unanimous proclamation of Brie as '*le roi
des fromages*'. The Brie in question was Brie de Meaux. The term
Brie covers a small family of cheeses, nowadays much depleted,
but all of which at one time carried the name of the particular
place where they were made. All are soft, unpressed, naturally
drained cows' milk cheeses with white rind flora, moulded into
large flat discs and ripened for three to four weeks. The family
name is that of the area in the *département* of Seine-et-Marne
where they originated and where the best ones are still made.
Nowadays Brie is made all over France and in many other
countries as well. There are numerous modern variations on the
traditional cheese, such as herb- and pepper-flavoured Bries
and versions with and/or white internal moulds. The
classic farm-made Bries of Brie itself are regrettably becoming
overshadowed by their more glamorous descendants.

All Bries should be full-flavoured, fruity and mildly tangy.
Ideally, the paste is rich, glossy and straw-coloured. It should be
plump and smooth but not runny. Avoid cheeses with a hard,
chalky centre and any that are liquefying. The rind should be
firm but tender, not hard or sticky. The smell should be clean
and pleasantly mouldy. Cheeses that smell of ammonia are
dangerously overripe and should not be eaten. Always buy Brie
cut from a whole cheese.

> *O my sweet heart, I send to you*
> *This delectable Brie de Meaux*
> *Which I chose with loving care*
> *To show you how your absence*
> *Has made me so unhappy*
> *That I have quite lost my appetite.*
> *So I give it to you.*
> *What a sacrifice it is for me!*
>
> Charles d'Orléans (1407)

Brie de Coulommiers see *Coulommiers*

Brie Laitier   🌼 ᠍🐄 40–50%   ᠍🧀 2–3kg (4–7lb)   🅐

The commercial version of Brie made from pasteurized milk,
both throughout France and in other countries as well. The rind
flora should be perfectly white with possibly some browning at
the edges. The interior is generally paler in colour than most
farmhouse cheeses. Ripened for about three weeks. Often sold
pre-packed in wedge-shaped boxes. See *Brie*

Brie de Meaux ★   🌼 ᠍🐄 45%   ᠍🧀 2.6kg (5½lb)   🅑

Brie *fermier* made in the Île de France from unpasteurized milk.
The rind is darker with more red-brown coloration than is
acceptable in Brie Laitier. Very fruity. Ripened for five to six
weeks. Protected by an *appellation d'origine*. See *Brie*

Brie de Melun Affiné 🎴 🐄 45% ⬡ 1.5kg (3lb) 🐑
Brie *fermier* made in the Île de France from unpasteurized milk.
Very dark rind with traces of white. Fairly firm, golden paste,
strong smelling and tangy, ripened for about seven weeks. The
mould, *Penicillium candidum*, develops naturally on the surface.
The strongest of the Bries, it is the original from which all the
others have descended. Protected by an *appellation d'origine*.
See *Brie*

Brie de Melun Frais 🎴 🐄 45% ⬡ 1.5kg (3lb) 🐑
Brie de Melun eaten unripened, sometimes available *bleu*,
which means that it is coated with powdered charcoal.

Brie de Montereau
🎴 🐄 40–45% ⬡ 400g–1kg (14oz–2lb) 🐑
Brie *fermier* made in the Île de France from unpasteurized milk.
A variety of Brie de Melun Affiné but smaller in size and ripened
for six weeks. Also called Ville-Saint-Jacques.

Brillat-Savarin 🎴 🐄 75% ⬡ 500g (18oz) 🐑
Soft, triple-cream cheese made in Forges-les-Eaux, Normandy.
Mild with a rich buttery paste and a light bloomy rind.

Brin d'Amour 🍂 🐑 45% ⬁ 600g (21oz) 🐑
Firm, aromatic, dryish cheese from Corsica. Ripened for three
months on a bed of herbs. The rind is grey and covered with
sprigs of rosemary and savory.

Briquette see *Neufchâtel*

Brisegoût
Whey cheese made in Savoie as a by-product of the making of
Beaufort. It is eaten either fresh or ripened when it becomes
hard, brittle and extremely piquant. Also called Brisco, Brisego.

Broccio, Brocciu
Fresh Corsican cheese once made from the whey by-product of
Sartenais but which now increasingly uses a proportion of
whole or skimmed milk. Made from ewes' milk (or occasionally
goats') it looks and tastes very much like Italian Ricotta. It can
also be dried and ripened for several months, when it becomes
sharp and tangy. Also called Bruccio, Brucciu.

Brousse du Rôve 🐑 🐄 45% 🐑
Fresh cheese made mostly on farms in Provence. Snowy white,
very mild and creamy. Drained and usually sold in wicker
baskets.

Bruccio see *Broccio*

Cabécou 🍂 🐑 45% ⬡ 40g (1½oz) 🐑
The name, a diminutive of *chèvre*, applies to several tiny, flat,
goats' milk cheeses made in Aquitaine. They are ripened for
about a month and range from semi-soft to firm. The flavour is
generally fairly pronounced. Occasionally made with ewes'
milk, or a mixture of cows' and goats' milk.

Cachat 🐑 🐄 45–50% 🐑
Fresh, white cheese from Provence made from the milk of
animals grazed on the slopes of Mont Ventoux. Goats' milk may
occasionally be used instead of ewes'. Very sweet and delicate

when fresh but sometimes used when ripe in the local version of Fromage Fort, once described as *fromage frénétique*. Also called Tomme de Mont Ventoux.

Caillada de Vouillos see *Tomme de Brach*

Caillebotte

Fresh, soft, rennet-curd cheese which can be made from any type of milk depending on the area. In the Basque country it will be ewes' milk, in Brittany cows' milk, in Poitou probably goats' milk. Farmhouse made, particularly in summer. Usually unsalted. Sold by weight or packed in earthenware jars or wicker baskets. The name comes from *caillé*, curdled milk. Also called Jonchée.

Camargue 🍂 🌙 45% ⬭ 60g (2oz) ◐

Ewes' milk cheese made in the Camargue in springtime. Flavoured with thyme and bay and eaten fresh. Also called Tomme Arlésienne or Tomme de Camargue.

Cambrai see *Boulette de Cambrai*

Camembert ★ ⏻ 🌙 45–50% ⬭ 250g (9oz) ◉

One of the three great Normandy cheeses, Camembert, in name at least, is relatively young in cheesemaking terms—a mere 280 years old. As a type it is certainly much older. The Pays d'Auge, still the best source of good Camembert, was known for its cheese as far back as the 11th century. ('*Fromages d'angelons*', ancestors of Pont l'Evêque, were mentioned in the *Roman de la Rose* [1236].) In 1702, 90 years before Mme Harel was credited with the 'invention' of Camembert, it was mentioned, along with Livarot, as being sold in the market at Vimoutiers. But Mme Harel did for Camembert what Mrs Paulet did for Stilton: she refined the recipe and launched it into the wider world. Like Mrs Paulet, she passed her secrets on to her daughter, whose husband, Victor Paynel, presented one of his wife's best cheeses to Napoleon III. With the royal seal of approval, the future of Camembert was assured. But two further developments were essential to its subsequent spectacular commercial success. One was the invention of the chipwood box in the 1890s. (Previously the cheeses were wrapped in sixes in paper and straw and rarely survived distances farther than Paris.) The second was the introduction in 1910 of *Penicillium candidum*, the snowy white mould which is sprinkled or sprayed on the surfaces of the cheeses. Previously, Camembert rinds were often blue.

Camembert is now made in enormous quantities in virtually every country in Europe and in the United States. In France it accounts for over 20 per cent of total cheese production. Most of this is factory-made from pasteurized milk and whatever the merits of these cheeses, they simply do not compare with the traditional hand-made Normandy cheeses using unpasteurized milk from local herds. These are in season from the end of spring through to the autumn. Check the label for the words *fromage fermier, lait cru* or *non pasteurisé* and the initials V.C.N.—*Véritable Camembert de Normandie*. If it also says Pays d'Auge, so much the better. The rind should be smooth and supple, the creamy white mould flecked with red, not cracked, crumpled or sticky. The paste should be plump and pale golden in colour with no chalky or greyish patches. It should not be runny or sunken in the middle. The smell should be clean and lightly fruity with no trace of ammonia.

The absence of information to the contrary tells you this Camembert is made from pasteurized milk

Made in Normandy, it should therefore be a good cheese

Cantal ★   🏷 🐄 45% 🗌 30–50kg (66–110lb) 🍎 🐄
Probably the oldest French cheese (*c.* 2,000 years), made in the Auvergne from the milk of Salers or Aubrac cows and protected by an *appellation d'origine*. Unfortunately, good Cantal is rarely found outside France. Often thought of as the French Cheddar, is has a smooth, close-textured, yellow paste with a pleasant rather nutty flavour. The rind is dry, grey and powdery. It is a pressed uncooked cheese, ripened between three and six months. There are two types: Cantal Laitier, a pasteurized version made all year round in creameries, and Cantal Fermier, made in summer during the period of transhumance in mountain huts (*burons*) or *fruitières*. Cantal Fermier is especially prized and is usually matured for longer than the creamery type. It also tends to be heavier. The biggest ones are made near Salers. Cantal Laitier rarely weighs more than 35kg (77lb). There is also a 'baby' farmhouse Cantal, known as Cantalet or Cantalon, weighing about 10kg (22lb), which is made towards the end of summer when the milk supply is drying up and so is particularly rich and high in fat content. These cheeses are usually consumed on special occasions. Cantal is used a great deal in regional dishes. Also called Salers, Fourme de Cantal, Fourme de Salers.

(On Camembert)
In this class fall the great romantics, all of which under stress of emotion are apt to weep, run, and generally spread themselves. Temperamental as pears, they must be carefully watched.

    Edward & Lorna Bunyard THE EPICURE'S COMPANION

Caprice des Dieux   🏷 🐄 60% 180g (6oz) 🐄
Factory-made, oval, double-cream cheese with white rind flora and a mild flavour. Sold boxed.

Carré de Bonneville see *Pavé d'Auge*

Carré de Bray   🏷 🐄 45% 🗀 🐄
From the Pays de Bray, Normandy, a small, Neufchâtel-type cheese made in small dairies in spring and summer.

Carré de l'Est   🏷 🐄 40–50% 🗀 200g (7oz) 🐄
Camembert type from Champagne and Lorraine. Mostly factory-made from pasteurized milk. Mild but slightly salty.

45

The white rind flora should be smooth with no red or grey streaks. The export version is usually smaller. There is also a washed-rind variant with the same name.

Cendré

Generic term for small soft cheeses ripened in wood ash for about two months. They are often strong and pungent. Beech, poplar, vine stems or any other suitable timber provide the ashes. Shaped into small discs, truncated cones or pyramids with greyish-black rinds. Traditionally prepared for consumption by farm workers during the harvest period, particularly in Champagne.

Cendré d'Aisy see *Aisy*
Cendré des Ardennes see *Rocroi*
Cendré d'Argonne see *Noyers-le-Val*
Cendré des Riceys see *Riceys, Les*

Chabichou
45% 100g (3½oz)

An ancient Poitevin cheese shaped like a small flattened cone or cylinder and emphatically goaty in flavour and aroma. The farmhouse type, in season from the end of spring until late autumn, has a firm pale blue rind streaked with red. Chabichou Laitier, made in small dairies, has a white bloomy rind. Best in summer. Both types are ripened for between two and three weeks. The name (occasionally found as Cabichou, Cabrichiu and Chabi) comes from a local dialect word for 'goat' derived, according to some, from the Arabic *chebli* (it was at Poitiers that Charles Martel repelled the advance of the Saracens in 732). There is also a Chabichou Cendré. Locally the cheeses are often eaten unripened.

Chambarand
45% 150g (5oz)

Made in the Abbaye de Chambarand in Dauphiné, a gentle cheese with a creamy yellow paste and smooth golden rind. Also called Trappiste de Chambarand.

Champenois see *Riceys, Les*

Chaource
45–50% 500g (18oz)

Milky white smooth-pasted cheese with a dryish rather than creamy consistency. It has a thin covering of white rind flora closely covered with a paper wrapping. Named after a small village near Troyes, it has a pleasantly fruity lactic flavour. Made mostly in small dairies from whole unpasteurized milk. Best in summer and autumn. Protected by an *appellation d'origine*.

Charolais, Charolles

Small soft cheese made from goats' milk or a mixture of cows' and goats' milk near Charolles, Burgundy. Eaten fresh or ripened for a couple of weeks, when the rind becomes tough and grey-blue in colour and the flavour more pronounced. Used in the local Fromage Fort.

Chaumes
50% 1.5kg (3lb)

From the Dordogne, a cheese with a rich golden creamy paste and a tough yellowy brown rind. Made from pasteurized milk, it has a springy, rather elastic consistency and a full, nutty flavour. Watch out for hardening beneath the rind and avoid any cheese which looks murky or dull.

Chaumont   ♨ 🍶 45% 200g (7oz) ◗
Small farm-made washed-rind cheese from Champagne.
Russet-coloured and shaped like a truncated cone, it has a
rather tangy flavour but can be slightly bitter. Ripened for two
months.

Chèvre
The generic term for goats' milk cheeses, of which there are
innumerable local types and variations. By law, cheeses
described as *chèvre* or *pur chèvre* must be made entirely of goats'
milk and must contain at least 45 per cent fat. Cheeses using a
minimum of 25 per cent goats' milk mixed with cows' milk are
described as *mi-chèvre* and have a yellow band on the label.

Chèvre à la Feuille see *Mothe-Saint-Héray, La*

Chevret
Soft goats' milk cheese from Bugey in Franche Comté. Also
called Tomme de Belley, Saint-Claude.

Chevreton
The generic term for *chèvre* or *mi-chèvre* cheeses from Burgundy
and the Auvergne.

Chevreton de Mâcon see *Bouton-de-Culotte*

Chevrette   🐐 🍶 70% ⬭ 1kg (2lb) 🧀
Fresh double-cream cheese flavoured with garlic and herbs.

Chevrette des Beauges   🐐 🍶 45% ⊝ 1–2kg (2–4lb) ◗
Pressed, uncooked cheese from Savoie. Smooth, medium-
flavoured with a pale, thin, shiny rind.

Chevrotin des Aravis   🐐 🍶 45% ⊝ 500g (18oz) 🧀
A mild-flavoured pressed cheese with a firm grey-brown rind
made in Haute-Savoie. With Chevrette des Beauges and other
similar medium-ripened, semi-hard goats' milk cheeses made in
the area it is often sold simply as Tomme de Chèvre, or Tomme
de Chèvre de Savoie.

Chevrotin du Bourbonnais   🐐 🍶 45% 100g (3½oz) ◗
Small flattened cone with a thin, dryish, natural crust. Eaten
fresh or ripened for a couple of weeks. Mild to fairly strong
depending on age.

Chevru   ♨ 🍶 45% ⊝ 500g (18oz) ◗
Surface-ripened cheese similar to Coulommiers and made in
the Île-de-France.

Cîteaux   ♨ 🍶 45% ⊝ 1.5kg (3lb) 🧀
Pressed, washed-rind cheese made in the monastery of the same
name in Burgundy. Made from unpasteurized milk, it has a
clean, fairly tangy flavour. Lightly dotted with holes. Should
not be too smelly.

Claquebitou
Burgundian fresh goat cheese flavoured with herbs and garlic.

Cœur d'Arras
Heart-shaped, soft, washed-rind, cows' milk cheese with a fairly
strong flavour. Similar to Maroilles.

Cœur de Bray 🏠 🐄 45% 100–300g (3½–10oz) 🐐

A kind of heart-shaped Neufchâtel. Fruity with a faint lactic edge. From the Pays de Bray in Normandy.

Cœurmandie 🏠 🐄 45% 2kg (4lb) 🐐

Factory-made heart-shaped soft cheese with white rind flora.

Cœur Neufchâtel see *Cœur de Bray*

Comté ★ 🏠 🐄 45% ⬡ 38–40kg (84–88lb) 🐄 🐐

One of the French Gruyère family, a hard-pressed cooked cheese with a smooth golden paste lightly scattered with medium-sized round holes. A good Comté can be judged almost entirely by the size, shape and condition of these holes or 'eyes'. They should not be too numerous or too close together. They should be perfectly round, no bigger than the size of a small marble and just moist and glistening. Comté has a dark, tough, brushed rind and is stronger than Emmental with a rich fruitier flavour. Made in Franche Comté since ancient times, it developed out of the need for isolated farm communities, with distant markets, to make a cheese that would keep in good condition for as long as possible. Since such cheeses also required more milk than could possibly be yielded by small herds it also necessitated pooling the milk from several herds and making the cheeses co-operatively. Farmers transported their milk to these local co-operatives (*fruitières*) each day and the cheeses were made by specialist, often itinerant, cheese-makers. This economic structure persists in many places even today. It can be documented back to the 13th century and is original to Gruyère country. Most usually sold in France as Gruyère de Comté. Protected by an *appellation d'origine*.

Couhé-Vérac 🐄 🐄 45% ⬡ 200g (7oz) 🐐

Farm-made around Couhé-Vérac in Poitou. Sharp and smelly, it is ripened for three to four weeks. Wrapped in chestnut or plane-tree leaves. Occasionally a flat disc shape.

Coulommiers ★ 🏠 🐄 45–50% ⬡ 500g (18oz) 🐐

Sometimes called Petit Brie or Brie de Coulommiers and made, mostly in factories, in the same area as Brie. Much smaller in size and eaten younger, preferably as the surface mould is beginning to appear (after ripening for a month). At this stage the flavour is quite mild and delicate: allowed to ripen further it becomes increasingly reminiscent of Camembert. Slower ripening cheeses enriched with added cream can sometimes be found as can those made from unpasteurized milk. See *Fougéru*.

Cremet

Unsalted fresh cows' milk cheese eaten with sugar or salted with chopped herbs. The best is said to come from Anjou.

Crottins de Chavignol 🐄 🐄 45% ○ 70g (2½oz) 🐐

Tiny, hard, dry cheeses with black or grey-brown mouldy rinds made for winter consumption on remote farms in Berry. Horribly sharp and salty when fully aged and somewhat intimidating to all but the most dedicated. The name is hardly inviting: it means 'horse-droppings'. There is a milder, factory-made version which is rather more approachable. Protected by an *appellation d'origine*.

Curé see *Nantais*

Dauphin ☼ ◑ 50% ◖

Small washed-rind cheese similar to Maroilles but variously flavoured with pepper, cloves, tarragon and parsley. Moulded in various shapes—bar, oval, fish, crescent, heart, shield—it has a firm brownish rind and strong spicy flavour. Ripened between three and four months. Made in Flanders.

Délice de Saint-Cyr ☼ ◑ 75% ▱ 500g (18oz) ◖

Rich, mild, triple-cream cheese with white rind flora. Ripened for three weeks. Factory-made in the Île de France.

Demi-Baguette see *Baguette*

Demi-Sel ☼ ◑ 40% ▭ 60g (2oz) ◔

Originating in the Pays de Bray in 1872, a smooth, white, factory-made, fresh rennet-curd cheese from pasteurized milk.

Chèvre fermier means this is made wholly from goats' milk on the farm. Ripened elsewhere by an *affineur*

CROTTIN de CHAVIGNOL
CHÈVRE FERMIER
45% de MAT. GR.
AFFINÉ PAR
DENIZOT
CHAVIGNOL
18

De mat. gr. (de matière grasse) means fat content

13 million are made each year—and, presumably, eaten

Dreux ☼ ◑ 30% ▱ 500g (18oz) ◑

Rich, fruity cheese with white rind flora spotted with red and wrapped in chestnut leaves. Made from partly skimmed milk in small dairies in the Île de France. Also called Feuille de Dreux, Dreux à la Feuille, Fromage à la Feuille.

Echourgnac ☼ ◑ 45% ▱ 300g (10oz) ◑

Mild, pale yellow, monastery-made cheese from Aquitaine with pinpoint holes. Pressed and uncooked with a buff-coloured washed rind. Also called Trappiste d'Echourgnac.

Emmental Français
 ☼ ◗ 45% ◒ 45–100kg (99–220lb) ● ◖

More Emmental is made in France than in any other country, including Switzerland, yet little is exported. Production of Emmental in France was begun in the 19th century by Swiss cheesemakers. It is now made, mostly in factories, in Franche Comté and Savoie from raw and pasteurized milk. Aged between two and six months. The best is the matured cheese from mountain areas. See *Switzerland (Emmental)*

Entrammes ★ ☼ ◗ 40% ◒ 350g (12oz) ◖

Pressed, uncooked, monastery-made cheese from the Abbaye d'Entrammes, Maine, whose cheeses were once sold as 'Port-Salut' until the monks sold the name to a commercial enterprise. See *Port-du-Salut*

Epoisses ☼ ◑ 45% ◒ 450g (1lb) ◖

Smooth, pungent, washed-rind cheese made in Burgundy. Spicy, tangy and occasionally also flavoured with black pepper, cloves or fennel. It has a rich orange-red rind which is washed either in white wine or eau-de-vie-de-marc (a job which was at one time allocated to orphans or other children dependent on public welfare). Sold after one to three months' ripening. Also used in the local Fromage Fort.

Ercé see *Bethmale*

Esbareich
Pressed, uncooked Béarnaise ewes' milk cheese, ripened for three months.

Esterençuby see *Ardi-Gasna*

Excelsior 72% 200g (7oz) C
Invented in 1890, a double-cream Normandy cheese with white rind flora, very smooth, mild and delicate.

Explorateur ★ 75% 250g (9oz) B
Rich triple-cream cheese made in small dairies in the *département* of Seine-et-Marne. Virtually odourless with a light covering of snowy white mould. Mild flavour. Ripened for three weeks.

Feuille de Dreux see *Dreux*

Fin-de-Siècle
Double-cream cheese like Excelsior from the Pays de Bray.

Fondu au Raisin
Processed cheese made mostly from Emmental and impressed on the surface with toasted grape pips. Also called Fondu au Marc, Tomme au Raisin. See *Fromage Fondu*

Fontainebleau 60% C
Very light, factory-made, unsalted fresh cheese. White and fluffy, it uses whole pasteurized milk mixed with whipped cream. Served for dessert with sugar, fruit or fruit purée.

Fontal 45% 10kg (22lb) B
Cheese very like Italian Fontina and called Fontina until the Stresa Convention of 1951 limited the term to cheeses made in the Val d'Aosta. Made mostly in eastern France, especially along the Italian border. See *Italy* (*Fontal, Fontina*)

Fougéru
A type of Coulommiers ripened in fronds of bracken.

Fourme d'Ambert ★ 45% 2kg (4lb) B
Looks like a tall baby Stilton and has a similar rough brown-grey crust. A lightly pressed creamy white cheese marbled with dark blue-green veining. The paste should be smooth and fairly moist, tasting quite rich and tangy but not too bitter. Best in summer and autumn at about four to five months old. It is a cheese that, like Stilton, should be cut horizontally. It has also been similarly much abused in the past by the practice of pouring alcohol (eau-de-vie or port) into the centre of the cheese to moisten it. Made in the Livradois, Auvergne. Protected by an *appellation d'origine*.

Fourme de Brach see *Tomme de Brach*
Fourme de Cantal see *Cantal*

Fourme de Forez, Fourme de Montbrison, Fourme de Pierre-sur-Haute

All similar in most respects to Fourme d'Ambert. Fourme de Forez can be used as a generic term covering these and other related cheeses.

Fourme de Laguiole see *Laguiole*

Fourme de Rochefort ⚙ ➌ 45% ▢ 5–10kg (11–22lb) ●

In all respects except size similar to Cantal. Made on mountain farms in the Auvergne.

Fourme de Salers see *Cantal*

Fromage Blanc

Fresh rennet-curd cheese made from skimmed or whole cows' milk and with varying fat content. Used a great deal in cooking (the low fat variety is a favourite ingredient in the *nouvelle cuisine*). It can also be eaten as it is with sugar or seasoned with spices and herbs.

Fromage à la Crème

Fromage Blanc coated with cream.

Fromage du Curé see *Nantais*
Fromage à la Feuille see *Dreux*

From Cantal and Cheshire and goats' milk cheeses came a dull and muffled booming like a melody on the bass, against which the sudden little waves of the Neufchâtels, the Troyes and the Mont d'Ors raised their shrill cries. Then the smells began to run wild, mixing violently with one another, thickening with gusts of Port-Salut, Limbourg, Géromé, Maroilles, Livarot, Pont l'Evêque, little by little merging and mingling, broadening out into a single explosion of smells.

Emile Zola SAVAGE PARIS

Fromage Fondu

The generic term for processed cheese with a minimum fat content of 40 per cent and a maximum moisture content of 50 per cent. Processed cheese with a similar fat content but a maximum moisture content of 56 per cent must be described as *fromage à tartiner* or *fromage pour tartine*.

Fromage Fort

This is not cheese as such, but a preparation usually based on dessert cheese that is, perhaps, not quite perfect or that has become too old for consumption in the normal way. These cheeses are mashed up with various spices, alcohol—often white wine or eau-de-vie—grape must, oil and herbs, sealed in jars and steeped, or macerated, for varying amounts of time. The longer the fermentation period the stronger the flavour but even the mildest of them are impossibly sharp, especially for novices. For locals it is a case of the stronger the better. Eaten after meals or as a snack with a tot of some equally explosive beverage. Different cheeses are used in different parts of the country: goat cheeses in Lyonnais, Cachat in Provence,

Maroilles in Artois, Gruyère and Bouton-de-Culotte in Beaujolais. In Dauphiné it is called Pétafine (derived from the verb *pétafiner*, meaning to knock someone flat on the back).

Fromage Frais

Fresh (i.e. unripened) white acid- or rennet-curd cheese with varying fat content. Some are light, very soft, with almost a pouring consistency and are the basis for many local and family dishes. One of the most popular desserts is *cœur à la crème* in which the cheese is combined with a mixture of beaten egg white and sugar, drained in heart-shaped moulds and then served with a sprinkling of sugar and possibly cream or fruit or fruit purée. This type is usually sold in tubs under a variety of brand names of which Jockey and Bon Blanc are perhaps the best known. Firmer fattier types are Demi-Sel and Petit-Suisse. There are also double- and triple-cream fresh cheeses which must have a minimum fat content of 60 and 75 per cent respectively. They should all be eaten as soon as possible after buying.

Fromage Grand Murols see *Murol*
Fromage de Monsieur see *Monsieur Fromage*
Fromage de la Mothe see *Mothe-Saint-Héray, La*

Fromage à la Pie

Fresh cheese made from skimmed or partly skimmed cows' milk. In the Île de France a term for an unripened Brie or Coulommiers.

Fromage de Troyes see *Barberey*

Gaperon (Gapron) ★ 35% 300–500g (10–18oz)

Shaped like an upturned basin, a lightly pressed cheese made from skimmed milk or buttermilk. Flavoured with garlic or sometimes peppercorns. Made in farms and small factories in the Auvergne. Ripened for about two months. These cheeses used to be hung to ripen from the beams of the farmhouse kitchen, enabling visitors to gauge the family wealth by a stealthy glance at the number of Gaperons.

Gérômé 45% 400g–1.5kg (14oz–3lb)

Washed-rind cheese similar to Munster. Made in the Vosges mostly from pasteurized milk. Sometimes flavoured with cumin seeds and sold as Gérômé Anise.

Gien 45% 200g (7oz)

Farmhouse cheese using goats' milk or a mixture of cows' and goats' milk. It has a dry, blue-grey rind and is sometimes wrapped in plane-tree or chestnut leaves. It may also be ripened in wood ash.

Gournay 45% 100g (3½oz)

A type of small Camembert from the Pays de Bray, ripened for no more than a week. The rind has a light down and the flavour is fairly mild. Strictly speaking this is Gournay Affiné; Boursin is an industrialized fresh version.

Graçay 45% 500g (18oz)

Flattened cone-shaped cheese with a natural charcoal-covered rind. It has a mild goaty smell, with a medium flavour and the paste should be very white. Ripened for about six weeks. From the Arnon valley.

Grand Murols see *Murol*

Grand Rustique ☼ ☽ 50% ⊖ 1kg (2lb) **ᛒ**
Soft cheese with white rind flora made from unpasteurized milk. The paste is buttery yellow and almost foamy in consistency with a delicate flavour. Looks like a small Brie and sometimes sold as a Camembert *non pasteurisé*.

Grataron ◀ ➌ 45% ☐ 200g (7oz) **◐**
Pressed, uncooked, tangy cheese from Savoie. Dull brown washed rind, smooth paste.

Gris de Lille ☼ ☽ 45% ⊂⊃ 800g (28oz) **◐**
A type of Maroilles, extremely strong and pungent, ripened twice as long. Made in Flanders. Also called Vieux Lille, Maroilles Gris, Puant de Lille, Puant Macéré.

Gruyère
Gruyère in France is not one cheese but three—Emmental, Beaufort and Comté—of which Beaufort is perhaps closest in appearance and flavour to the authentic Swiss Gruyère. See *Beaufort, Comté, Emmental; Switzerland (Gruyère)*

Heilitz-le-Maurupt ☼ ☽ 30% ⊖ 200g (7oz) **◐**
Smooth, spicy cheese ripened in wood ash for about two months. Made from partly skimmed milk.

Igny ☼ ☽ 42% ⊖ 1–2kg (2–4lb) **◐**
A Saint-Paulin type made from unpasteurized milk. Also called Abbaye d'Igny, Trappiste d'Igny.

Iraty see *Ossau-Iraty-Brebis Pyrénées*
Jonchée see *Caillebotte*

Laguiole ★ ☼ ➌ 50% ☐ 50kg (110lb) **◕ ◐**
Superb hard-pressed cheese, related to Cantal, made in *burons*, small one-man chalets in the Aubrac mountains of Aquitaine, from the milk of Aubrac cattle. A much sought-after cheese which is still being made today by methods first documented in the 12th century. The paste is smooth, light golden yellow in colour, with a wonderful full fruity flavour. The rind is dry, hard and greyish-white to dark grey. Normally aged for about three months, although particularly good specimens are sometimes ripened for a further three months to produce a strong robust flavour. Also called Fourme de Laguiole, Laguiole-Aubrac. Protected by an *appellation d'origine*.

Langres ☼ ☽ 45% 200g (7oz) **◐**
Small yellowy brown, washed-rind cheese shaped like a sunken drum, made in Champagne. Strong and spicy.

Larron d'Ors ☼ ☽ 30% ⊂⊃ 250–700g (9–25oz) **◐**
A type of Maroilles made from partly skimmed milk. Quick ripening, about six to seven weeks. Strong-smelling and tangy.

Laruns ♥ ➌ 45% ⊖ 5–6kg (11–13lb) **◕ ◐**
Pressed, firm Pyrenean cheese ripened for two months for table use and longer, up to six months, for cooking. Odourless but with a full sheepy flavour. Related to similar cheeses made in the neighbouring Basque country. A factory-made cows' milk version is widely available under the name Pyrénées. The ewes'

milk types, which are infinitely preferable, are often sold under the generic name Pyrénées de Brebis.

Laumes ⏳ 🌢 45% ▱ 1kg (2lb) ●
Rare Burgundy washed-rind cheese. During the three-month ripening the rind is washed with water and occasionally with white wine or coffee, giving it an oddly smoky flavour.

Levroux 🍖 🌢 45% ●
Mild cheese similar to Valençay, like a flattened pyramid.

Lezay 🍖 🌢 45% ▭ 2kg (4lb) ♦
From Poitou, cheese with a smooth medium-flavoured white paste and a semi-hard creamy skin.

Livarot ★ ⏳ 🌢 40–45% ▱ 300–500g (10–18oz) ♦
One of the great Normandy cheeses and one of the oldest. Farmhouse production has now been almost entirely superseded by factory-made cheese. A washed-rind cheese with an assertive flavour and a smell to match, made from a mixture of skimmed evening and whole morning milk. Ripened in a warm, humid, unventilated environment for about three months. The rind should be a smooth, shiny brown and just moist, neither too dry nor too sticky. The paste should be golden and fairly springy. Avoid cheeses that are runny or sunken in the middle. The traditional drink with Livarot is the local cider or Calvados. Protected by an *appellation d'origine*.

Lormes 🍖 🌢 45% 200g (7oz)
Small blue-grey flattened cone with a delicate, pleasant flavour. Similar to Valençay. Occasionally *mi-chèvre*.

Lorraine ⏳ 🌢 40% ▱ 2–6kg (4–13lb) ●
A type of Gérômé but sold after only a month's ripening.

Lucullus
A term used for several triple-cream cheeses with white rind flora. See *Boursault*

Lusignan 🍖 🌢 45% ▱ 200g (7oz) 🍎 ●
Small, mild *chèvre*, barely ripened (about one to two weeks). Creamy and smooth, pure white in colour.

Magnum ⏳ 🌢 75% ▱ 500g (18oz) ◖
Triple-cream cheese from the Pays de Bray. Aged about three weeks. Similar to Brillat-Savarin, Excelsior.

Mamirolle ⏳ 🌢 40% ▱ 500g (18oz) ♦
Made in Franche Comté from pasteurized milk, a recently invented, lightly pressed, washed-rind cheese. Reminiscent of German Limburger but gentler in every respect.

Maroilles ★ ⏳ 🌢 40–50% ▱ 200–800g (7–28oz) ♦
The *pater familias* of Flemish washed-rind cheeses. Certainly one of the most ancient cheeses, invented in the 10th century by one of the monks at the abbey at Maroilles. Since then it has acquired a string of admirers and as many variations and imitations. The rind is reddish with a light damp sheen and should not be too sticky or too dry. The paste is a smooth pale yellow and, while certainly tangy, is rather more subtle in flavour than other similar cheeses. It should not be bitter or

chalky in texture. The smell is strong and full but not
ammoniacal. The ripening period lasts about four months.
Most Maroilles are still farmhouse-made. Smaller versions are
sold under the names Maroilles-Sorbais, -Mignon and -Quart.
Eaten as a dessert cheese and used to make Fromage Fort.
Protected by an *appellation d'origine*. See *Gris de Lille, Dauphin*

Meilleraye, La
Semi-hard pressed cows' milk cheese from Brittany.

Monsieur Fromage ★   🐄 🥛 60% ▭ 150g (5oz) 🧀
Rich, delicate double-cream cheese from Normandy. It has a
thick bloomy white rind and a creamy velvety yellow paste with
a superb fruity flavour. Eaten fresh after six weeks' ripening or
aged a little more so that the rind becomes slightly spotted with
reddish patches. Invented in the last century by the ap-
propriately named Monsieur Fromage. Also called Fromage de
Monsieur.

Mont-des-Cats   🐄 🥛 40% ⬭ 2kg (4lb) ◗
Monastery-made in Flanders. Similar to Saint-Paulin.

Montoire   🐐 🥛 45% 80g (3oz) ◗
Farmhouse cheese from the Loire valley. Small, blue-grey
flattened cone with a mild goaty aroma and mellow flavour.

Montrachet   🐐 🥛 45% ▭ 75g (2½oz) ◗
Small cylindrical goat cheese ripened for about a week in vine or
chestnut leaves and sold still wrapped in leaves. From the
département of Saône-et-Loire in Burgundy.

Montréal
A kind of Epoisses made on a small scale in the Serein valley.

Montrésor
A goat cheese similar to Sainte-Maure.

Montségur (Monségur)   🐄 🥛 45% ⬭ 3kg (7lb) 🧀
Factory-made, fairly tasteless pressed cheese from Ariège in the
foothills of the Pyrenees. It has a thin washed rind, artificially
blackened. Sometimes pepper flavoured.

Morbier   🐄 🥛 45% ⬭ 6–8kg (13–18lb) 🧀
An odd-looking cheese made in mountain chalets in the Juras
during the winter. The pale yellow smooth paste is divided
horizontally by a band of blue-black soot or powdered
charcoal. Traditionally the cheese was made partly from
morning milk and partly from evening milk coagulated
separately. The layer of soot protected the morning curds until
the evening curds were placed on top. A mellow cheese,
virtually odourless, with a light grey dry rind. Ripened for two
to three months. Best in spring.

Mothe-Saint-Héray, La   🐐 🥛 45% 200g (7oz) 🧀
One of several fine goat cheeses made in a variety of shapes in the
Poitevin town of the same name. It is ripened for a couple of
weeks between layers of vine- or plane-tree leaves and has a
fairly pronounced flavour and a smooth downy white rind. Also
called Fromage de la Mothe, Mothais, Chèvre à la Feuille.

Moyaux see *Pavé d'Auge*

Munster ★   🌡 🍶 40% 🧀 500g–1kg (18oz–2lb) 🐄

An ancient cheese from Alsace and the Vosges, supposedly first made by Irish monks who settled in the area in the 7th century. The cheese is red-skinned and very spicy and tangy with an emphatic aroma like all washed-rind cheeses. The paste is buttery yellow and very rich and creamy. In Alsace itself it is often eaten when younger and milder. The farmhouse type (Munster Fermier) is made in summer in the *hautes chaumes* (literally 'high stubble') of the Vosges mountains, and in winter on farms lower down the slopes. Munster Laitier is made all year round from pasteurized milk. The ripening period is one to three months depending on the size of the cheese. Best between November and May especially, according to enthusiasts, with hot baked jacket potatoes. Protected by an *appellation d'origine*. See *Germany* (*Münster*)

Muntanacciu

Corsican ewes' milk cheese ripened two to three months.

Mur de Barez

Rare cheese made from goats' milk whey.

Murol   🌡 🍶 45% 470g (1lb) 🐄

A mild, pressed, disc-shaped cheese with a small hole in the middle. The washed rind is pinkish-brown and fairly resilient. Made with pasteurized milk in the Auvergne. A variation of Saint-Nectaire, also called Grand Murols.

Nantais   🌡 🍶 40% 🧀 200g (7oz) 🐄

The most important Breton cheese, invented in the last century by a priest from the Vendée. A pressed, uncooked cheese with a full flavour and pronounced smell. Golden, light brown, rubbery rind. Usually made from pasteurized milk. Also called Curé, Fromage du Curé.

Neufchâtel ★   🌡 🍶 45% 🐄

Famous rich creamy cheese eaten fresh or ripened from the Pays de Bray, Normandy. The curds are finely milled, making the consistency particularly smooth and homogeneous. Nowadays mostly factory-made although farmhouse versions can still be found. Fresh Neufchâtel is white with a faint sourish lactic flavour and a bloomy white rind. Neufchâtel Affiné is darker, more golden in colour, the rind shows traces of red-brown pigmentation and the flavour becomes much more pronounced and rather salty. It is moulded in a variety of shapes—heart, roll, loaf, square—known as Cœur, Bondon, Briquette and Carré. The ripened type goes particularly well with strong, full-bodied wines. Protected by an *appellation d'origine*.

Niolo   🌡 🍶 45% 🧀 500g (18oz) 🐑

Farm-made in the mountains of Corsica, a strong, fairly coarse, tangy, ewes' milk cheese (occasionally made with goats' milk). It has a dull, whitish, brine-washed rind and a yellowy paste after three months' ripening. Also eaten fresh and mild.

Noyers-le-Val   🌡 🍶 30% 🧀 200g (7oz) 🐄

Low-fat, fairly strong, firm cheese ripened in ashes for two to three months. From Argonne, between Lorraine and Champagne. Produced seasonally in summer and autumn on farms to coincide with harvest and the *vendange* (grape-gathering). Extremely rare. Also called Cendré d'Argonne.

Oelenberg 45% 1–1.5kg (2–3lb)

Gentle cheese with an elastic golden yellow paste and a smooth, supple rind. Ripened for two months. Made all year round, initially in the monastery of Oelenberg in Alsace and now in small dairies in the area. Also called Trappiste d'Oelenberg.

Oléron 45%

Fresh ewes' milk cheese that has all but disappeared. Very mild, white, soft and creamy. Farm-made on the island of Oléron, Aunis. Should be eaten with the local white wine.

Olivet Bleu ★ 45% 300g (10oz)

A light, almost sweet-flavoured cheese reminiscent of Coulommiers. The white rind flora has a blue tinge and arises naturally during the one-month ripening period. Sold wrapped in leaves. There is also an Olivet Cendré, which is cured for three months in the ashes of vine stems and has a much stronger flavour. Olivet au Foin is ripened in hay.

Oloron 45% 4kg (9lb)

Pressed, semi-hard ewes' milk cheese made in the Basque country. Eaten fairly young and mild or aged, when it develops a sharper taste. The cheese fair held every September in Oloron-Sainte-Marie is the best source.

Orrys, Les 45% 10–12kg (22–26lb)

Pressed, uncooked, full-flavoured cheese once made with ewes' milk. Has a rich smooth golden paste and is fine and fruity, reminiscent of a good Italian Fontina. The animals are grazed on exceptionally fine summer pastures in the mountains of Ariège. Sometimes spiced with peppercorns or pimento.

The fox and the crow, a reference to La Fontaine's fable:

Maître Corbeau sur un arbre perché, Tenait en son bec un fromage . . .

FROMAGE GRAND MUROLS
FABRIQUE EN AUVERGNE
J. BERIOUX
63800 - COURNON-D'AUVERGNE
45% DE MATIÈRES GRASSES
POIDS NET MINIMUM A L'EMBALLAGE: 470g COLORANT DE LA CROUTE E 172

French labels must specify any artificial colouring, in this case, of the rind

Ossau-Iraty-Brebis Pyrénées ★ 50% 4–5kg (9–11lb)

Made in Béarn and the Basque provinces in farms and small dairies by traditional methods. This is the original authentic Pyrenean ewes' milk cheese, now widely imitated. Lightly pressed, uncooked with a golden springy paste scattered with small irregular holes and openings. The rind is smooth orange-yellow to brown, the flavour delicate to full and mellow according to age. Ripened for at least three months. Older drier cheeses are used for grating. Protected by an *appellation d'origine*. See *Pyrénées*

Ourde
Ewes' milk cheese similar to Esbareich. Made in Languedoc.

Oust, Oustet see *Bethmale*

Pannes Cendré   🗘 🕲 20–30% ▢ 200g (7oz) ◗
Made from skimmed milk and ripened in wood ash for three months. Similar to Olivet Cendré and made in farms and small dairies in Orléans.

Parfait
Brand name for a triple-cream cheese made near Forges-les-Eaux. Much like Excelsior but ripened a little longer.

Parthenay
Soft, fresh goats' milk cheese from Poitou.

Passé l'An   🗘 ❥ 28% ▢ 35–40kg (77–88lb) ● ●
An imitation of Italian Grana cheese. Made from pasteurized skimmed milk and developed during World War II when imports of Italian cheese were proscribed. The name derives from the fact that the cheeses must be aged for at least a year.

Patay   🗘 🕲 45% ▢ 500g (18oz) ◗
Similar to Olivet. Blued naturally or ripened in wood ash.

Pavé d'Auge   🗘 🕲 50% ▱ 800g (28oz) ◖
Washed-rind cheese which looks like a much larger Pont l'Evêque. Fairly firm yellow paste with lots of small elliptical holes. Strong-tasting, almost bitter. The rind is thick, resilient, ridged, dull orange in colour and smeared with powdery white moulds. Ripened for two to four months. Made in the Pays d'Auge. (*Pavé*, 'slab' or 'paving stone'). Also called Pavé de Moyaux, Carré de Bonneville.

Pavé Blésois
Fairly large goats' milk cheese. Usually coated in wood ash.

Pavé de Moyaux see *Pavé d'Auge*

Pavé de Valençay
A *chèvre* similar to an ordinary Valençay but very much larger.

Pelardon   🐐 🕲 45% ▢ 100g (3½oz) ◖
Small, white, barely ripened goats' milk cheese from Languedoc. Odourless, with a very agreeable nutty flavour and the typical goaty aftertaste. There are several variations, such as Pelardon d'Anduze, some flavoured with herbs. All are basically simple rustic cheeses and are still made almost entirely on local farms. According to an old wives' tale, Pelardon is an effective cure for jaundice.

Perail, Peral
Fresh ewes' milk cheese ripened on straw. From Rouergue.

Persillé des Aravis   🐐 🕲 45% ▢ 1kg (2lb) ◗
Blue-veined farmhouse cheese from Haute-Savoie. It has a rough grey-brown natural rind and is sharp and rather salty. Ripened for about two months. Probably the best of the few blue-veined goat cheeses. Also called Persillé de Thônes, Persillé du Grand-Bornand, Persillé de la Clusaz.

Persillé du Mont-Cenis   🐄 45% ⬜ 8kg (18lb) ●
Blue-veined cheese using a mixture of cows' and goats' milk.
Lightly pressed with a firm greyish crust. Ripened for about
three months. Farmhouse-made in Savoie.

Persillé de Thônes see *Persillé des Aravis*

Petit Bessay   🍶 🐄 40% ⊖ 200g (7oz) ●
Quick-ripened farmhouse cheese. Mild to medium flavour.

Petit Brie see *Coulommiers*

Petit-Suisse   🍶 🐄 60% ⬜ 30–60g (1–2oz) ▲
Fresh double-cream cheese made with pasteurized milk.
Unsalted, very bland, with a moist, almost watery consistency.
Made all over France. Invented in the mid 19th century by a
Mme Heroult who was Swiss, hence the name. There is also a
triple-cream version.

Picadou
Kind of Cabécou made from ewes' or goats' milk and wrapped
in leaves. Very strong flavour. See *Rocamadour*

Picodon de Dieulefit   🐐 🐄 45% ⊖ 75g (2½oz) ●
From Dauphiné. Ripened for two months and then steeped for
a subsequent month in a vat of white wine.

Picodon de Saint-Agrève   🐐 🐄 45% ⊖ 100g (3½oz) ●
Quick-ripened sharpish small goat cheese from Vivarais.

Pierre-qui-Vire   🍶 🐄 45% ⊖ 200g (7oz) ●
Washed-rind tangy cheese from the Benedictine monastery of
La Pierre-qui-Vire, Burgundy. Smelly with a pinkish-red
smooth rind. Can be eaten fresh. Similar to Epoisses.

Pierre-sur-Haute
Blue-veined cheese similar to Fourme d'Ambert and also made
in the Auvergne.

Pipo Crem'
Semi-soft log-shaped blue-veined cheese similar to Bleu de
Bresse.

Pithiviers au Foin see *Bondaroy au Foin*
Poivre d'Ane see *Banon*

Poivre d'Auvergne   🍶 🐄 50% ⊖ 4kg (9lb) ●
Recently invented cheese with a smooth, dense, pale yellow
paste and a hard, black, shiny, artificial rind. Creamy, mild and
flavoured with crushed black peppercorns.

Pont l'Evêque ★   🍶 🐄 40–50% ⬭ 350g (12oz) ●
Probably the oldest of the Normandy cheeses, known to the
author of the *Roman de la Rose* as Angelot. Since the 1600s it has
been called Pont l'Evêque after the market town in Calvados
which became the principal distribution point. Still made
mostly on farms from unpasteurized milk, although factory
production is beginning to gather momentum. It is a soft, rich,
golden-yellow cheese with a rind that is yellowy gold or light tan
depending on the finishing. During the two-month ripening
period the rind may be brine-washed or simply brushed. The

milk should be coagulated as soon as possible after milking. (Traditionally two batches of cheeses were made, one from morning and one from evening milk.) The curds are divided into large blocks (one per cheese) rather than cut, and these blocks are then lightly drained for ten minutes before being placed in square moulds. The smell should be moderately strong but not offensive and the flavour rich and tangy without being sharp or bitter. Larger versions (Pavé de Moyaux, Pavé d'Auge) are ripened for four to six months and are considerably stronger. Avoid cheeses where the rind is brittle or cracked. Protected by an *appellation d'origine*.

Port-du-Salut, Port-Salut 🐄 🐄 45% ⊖ 1–2kg (2–4lb) **6**
The archetypal monastery cheese, lightly pressed with a tawny washed rind and smooth, springy, semi-soft paste. The flavour is full and mellow with a slight edge but not so tangy as other washed-rind cheeses. Port-du-Salut originated in the early 19th century at the abbey of Entrammes near Laval in the *département* of Mayenne. The abbey was the home of a community of Cistercian monks from 1233 until the Revolution, when it and many other similar establishments were forced to close and their occupants flee the country. In 1815 a group of Trappists, returning from exile in Switzerland, were allowed to make use of the abbey, which they renamed L'Abbaye de Notre Dame de Port-du-Salut. Their cheeses, influenced by Swiss techniques, became well-known in Parisian markets under the description *façon Port-du-Salut*. Such was the demand for these cheeses that they were widely imitated and the monks took steps to protect their product. Finally in 1938 the name Port-Salut was legally defined as the trade mark of Port-du-Salut cheeses and cheeses with either name are the same. This mark was sold after World War II to a commercial enterprise but the monks continued making their own cheeses, which are now sold under the name of the abbey, Entrammes. See *Entrammes, Saint-Paulin*

Pouligny-Saint-Pierre 🐐 🐄 45% 200g (7oz) **O**
Pyramid-shaped with a natural blue-grey rind and a tangy flavour. Ripened a month, sometimes wrapped in leaves. Protected by an *appellation d'origine*.

Pourly 🐐 🐄 45% ▢ 300g (10oz) **O**
Recently invented, fairly delicate-flavoured goat cheese made in small dairies in Burgundy. It has a blue-grey natural rind, and a smooth white paste. Ripened for a month.

Poustagnac
Fresh cheese made from cows', ewes', or goats' milk and flavoured with peppercorns or pimento. From Les Landes.

Providence see *Bricquebec*
Puant de Lille, Puant Macéré see *Gris de Lille*

Pyrénées
Two types of cheese are sold under this designation. One is a factory-made cows' milk cheese, with a shiny black thin rind and a firm springy yellow paste punctuated by many small holes. The flavour is mild and rather indifferent. The other is a ewes' milk cheese with a firm golden orange rind, a very smooth dense paste with few holes and a tangy flavour. Related to the classic Pyrenean ewes' milk cheeses such as Ardi-Gasna, Esbareich, Ossau-Iraty-Brebis and Laruns.

Ramequin de Lagnieu

Small cylindrical farmhouse goats' cheese made in Bugey. Eaten after two or three weeks' ripening, when it is firm and tangy, or aged further and used grated for *fondu bugiste*.

Reblochon ★   ☼ ◗ 50% ⊟ 240–500g (8–18oz) ◖

One of the magnificent cheeses from the mountains of Haute-Savoie, in particular the Aravis Massif centring on Thônes. Reblochon uses the pasteurized or unpasteurized milk of Tarentaise cattle and is made by farms, *fruitières* and large dairies. It is a lightly pressed, scalded cheese with a supple creamy paste and firm pinkish-brown washed rind. The flavour is mild, fruity and absolutely delicious. It gets rather bitter as it ages. Usually ripened for about five weeks. Sold between two paper-thin wooden discs. The name comes from a dialect word for second milking which refers not to the second milking of the day but to the particularly rich milk that is left in the cow towards the end of a milking. This was very often appropriated by the cowherds themselves. It would be left in the cow until the farm proprietor had safely departed from checking the milk yield and then used to make their own cheese, namely Reblochon. Protected by an *appellation d'origine*.

Made in a *fruitière* run by a farmers' co-operative. It bears the *appellation d'origine* —the genuine article

Riceys, Les   ☼ ◗ 30–40% ⊟ 300g (10oz) ◖

Made in Champagne from skimmed milk and ripened in the ashes of vine stems for one to two months. Fairly strong. Also called Cendré des Riceys, Champenois.

Rigotte   ◗ 40–50% ⊟ 70g (2½oz) ◖

Very small round cheese made in Lyonnais and the Auvergne from cows' milk or a mixture of cows' and goats' milk. Usually ripened for no more than a couple of weeks. Fairly mild to tangy in flavour depending on the milk and the finishing. Some are ripened naturally, some steeped in white wine or oil. Some are artificially coloured. The name is probably a corruption of *recuite*, meaning 'recooked', or of the name Ricotta, meaning the same in Italian. Both words indicate that the cheeses are, or at least were, whey cheeses, though nowadays full milk is used. Rigotte de Condrieu, Rigotte des Alpes and Rigotte de Pélussin are the best known.

Rocamadour   ◗ 45% ⊟ 30g (1oz) ◖

Tiny cheeses made in Aquitaine from ewes' or goats' milk and ripened for one week. The same cheeses wrapped in leaves and aged for a further period in stoneware pots become extremely strong and are then known as Picadou.

Rochefort see *Fourme de Rochefort*

Rocroi
20–30% 350g (12oz)

Square or disc-shaped farmhouse cheese made from skimmed milk in Champagne. Ripened in wood ash for one to two months. Fairly strong to very strong depending on age. Also called Cendré des Ardennes, Rocroi Cendré.

Rogeret des Cévennes
45% 85g (3oz)

Tangy small cheese with a strong goaty smell, made in Languedoc in summer and autumn. Ripened for about a month. The reddish skin is artificially coloured.

Rollot
45% 200g (7oz)

Round or heart-shaped washed-rind cheese from Picardy. Soft and supple with a smooth, moist, orange-red surface, it is strong-smelling and has a pronounced tang. Ripened for two months. Similar to Maroilles.

A Picardy cheese but this one comes from Normandy

Note the higher than usual fat content – a result possibly of superior milk

Roquefort ★
45% 2.5kg (5½lb)

A cheese with champions as diverse as Pliny, Charlemagne and Casanova arouses formidable expectations. Its aphrodisiac qualities, predictably emphasized by Casanova, have yet to undergo properly conducted scientific experiments, but its gastronomic merit remains unchallenged to this day. Even people who do not like blue cheeses generally like Roquefort. At its best it is extraordinarily delicate and subtle with none of the harsh overtones which typify many other blues. It has been made in Les Causses for thousands of years and its makers have regularly ensured that their product is legally defined and protected. They were first granted a monopoly on its making in 1411 and this has been confirmed at frequent intervals ever since, culminating in the Stresa Convention of 1951. It is now protected by an *appellation d'origine*.

Roquefort is made from the milk of the Larzac breed of sheep and ripened in the caves of Combalou. Some cheeses made from Corsican milk are brought to the same caves to be ripened, extending the availability of the cheeses over virtually a whole year. The caves, ventilated by currents of air known as *fleurines*, provide ideal conditions for the development of the mould, now defined as *Penicillium roquefortii*. This mould, which once grew naturally, is now partly induced by being sprinkled in powdered form on the curds as they are ladled into the moulds. The cheeses are then pierced with steel needles during the three-month ripening period. For the final part of this time the cheeses are closely wrapped in tin foil so that the finished product has virtually no rind. The veining (more green than blue) should be evenly distributed throughout the cheese and the paste should be creamy white and rather buttery. The sheepish origins of the cheese should be easily detectable in both flavour and aroma.

Each cheese, foil-wrapped, carries a label depicting a sheep printed in red ink. Unfortunately many exported Roqueforts tend to be oversalted to improve their keeping qualities. Those sold in France are much the best. Roquefort is eaten as a dessert cheese and also used in spreads and salad dressings.

Rouy 🐄 🥛 ⬜ 200g (7oz) ◐
Like a small Munster, factory-made in Burgundy.

Ruffec 🐐 🥛 45% ⬭ 250g (9oz) ◐
Poitevin goat cheese which develops a natural dry bluish rind after one month's ripening. It has a smooth, glossy and fairly mild paste. Sometimes eaten fresh.

Sableau 🐐 🥛 45% 200g (7oz) ◐
Fresh white triangular cheese from Poitou. Moist and mildly goaty. Also called Trois Cornes, Trébèche.

Saingorlon see *Bleu de Bresse*

Saint-Benoît 🐄 🥛 40% ⬭ 400g (14oz) ◐
Farmhouse-made from partly skimmed milk in Orléans. Pale yellow with a fruity flavour. Ripened two to four weeks.

Saint-Claude see *Chevret*

Saint-Florentin 🐄 🥛 45% ⬭ 500g (18oz) ◖
Washed-rind cheese from Burgundy similar to Epoisses. It has a rich, ruddy colour, a strong smell and a spicy tang.

Saint-Gelais
Farmhouse *chèvre* similar to Chabichou, from Poitou.

Saint-Gildas 🐄 🥛 75% ▯ 200g (7oz) ◖
Triple-cream cheese from Brittany made with pasteurized milk. Mild and creamy, with a smooth white, bloomy rind.

Saint-Lizier
A type of Bethmale made in Ariège. Also called Saint-Girons.

Saint-Maixent 🐐 🥛 45% ⬭ 250g (9oz) ◐
Rare Poitevin cheese with a natural blue-grey rind, strong flavour and a penetrating goaty smell. Ripened six weeks.

Saint-Marcellin ★ 🐄 🥛 50% ⬭ 90g (3oz) ◖
Used to be made with goats' milk but now a cows' milk cheese from Dauphiné. Fairly mild and unpressed. The rind is thin and covered with a light blue mould. Sometimes wrapped in chestnut leaves. It is *à point* when the paste just clings to the blade of the knife. Best between April and September.

Sainte-Marie 🐄 🥛 45% ▯ 400g (14oz) ◖
Fresh white rennet-curd cheese from Burgundy. Very bland.

Sainte-Maure ★ 🐐 🥛 45% ⬯ 300g (10oz) ◖
Both *fermier* and *laitier* types are available. Made in Poitou and Touraine, a soft and creamy cheese with a full goaty flavour. Crusted with a downy white rind tinged with pink. Recognizable by the length of straw through the centre of the cheese (not always present in the factory-made variety). There is also a Sainte-Maure Cendré.

Saint-Nectaire ★

🐄 ⊘ 45% ⊟ 800g–1.5kg (28oz–3lb) ● 🅑

From the Dore mountain in the Auvergne, an ancient cheese made twice a day from morning and evening milk separately. Pressed for 24 hours and ripened on rye straw for two months. The natural crust shows patches of red, yellow and white moulds. It has a firm, golden paste with a gentle mellow flavour. The *fermier* type has an oval plaque on the crust. The factory version has a rectangular plaque. A good melting cheese and a good keeping one. Protected by an *appellation d'origine*.

Saint-Paulin

🐄 ⊘ 40% ⊟ 1.5–2kg (3–4lb) 🅐

A factory-made descendant of Port-du-Salut made from pasteurized milk throughout the year all over France. It has a smooth, bright orange rind and a buttery yellow interior. A pressed uncooked cheese, it is ripened for about two months and has a mild, bland flavour. Also made in other countries.

Saint-Rémy

🐄 ⊘ 40% ▱ 200g (7oz) 🅓

Lightly pressed washed-rind cheese similar to Gérômé. It has a mid-brown rind, springy pale yellow paste, pronounced smell and a tangy flavour. From Franche Comté and Lorraine.

Salers see *Cantal*

Sancerre

Small goats' milk cheese made in Berry.

Sarriette, La

Soft *chèvre* or *mi-chèvre* coated with savory. See *Banon*

Sartenais (Sarteno)

⊘ ◯ 1–2kg (2–4lb) ● 🅓

Rustic Corsican ewes' or goats' milk cheese ripened for three months or aged further for grating. See *Broccio*

Sassenage see *Bleu de Sassenage*

Savaron

🐄 ⊘ 45% ⊟ 1.5kg (3lb) 🅓

Made from pasteurized milk in the Auvergne. A pressed, uncooked cheese similar to Saint-Nectaire Laitier.

Selles-sur-Cher ★

🐐 ⊘ 45% ⊟ 100g (3½oz) 🅓

Sweet, nutty cheese from Berry, ripened for three weeks and covered with powdered charcoal and salt. The surface is blue-black and the paste white, smooth and close-textured. Protected by an *appellation d'origine*.

Semussac

Small, rich, creamy fresh cows' milk cheese from Aquitaine.

Septmoncel see *Bleu de Septmoncel*
Sorbais see *Maroilles*

Sospel

A cows' milk cheese from Nice, like a huge Tomme de Savoie.

Soumaintrain

🐄 ⊘ 45% ⊟ 350g (12oz) 🅓

Washed-rind farmhouse cheese from Burgundy. Ripened for six to eight weeks. Between Saint-Florentin and Munster in flavour and aroma. Also eaten younger when white and creamy.

Tamié ☒ 🝕 40% ⊝ 1kg (2lb) ◐

A Savoyard monastery cheese made near Annecy. Pressed and uncooked with a pale ochre washed rind, a springy golden paste and a mild flavour. Also called Trappiste de Tamié.

Tartare

Herb-flavoured factory-produced soft cheese made in Périgord from pasteurized cows' milk.

Thiviers

Small goats' cheese similar to Cabécou.

Tomme d'Abondance see *Abondance*
Tomme d'Aligot see *Tomme Fraîche*

Tomme des Allues 🝕 🝕 45% ⊝ 3–4kg (7–9lb) ◐

Made in the Tarentaise mountains of Savoie. A pressed, uncooked, mild goats' milk cheese with a pale, dull yellow, smooth rind and smooth buttery paste.

Tomme Arlésienne see *Camargue*

Tomme de Belleville ☒ 🝕 30% ⊝ 1.5–3kg (3–7lb) ◐

Pressed, uncooked cheese made in Savoie, from skimmed milk.

Tomme de Belley see *Chevret*

Tomme de Brach 🝕 🝕 45% ☐ 500g (18oz) ◐

Farmhouse ewes' milk cheese ripened for two to four months. Rather heavy and coarse. Sometimes blue-veined. Also called Caillada de Vouillos, Fourme de Brach.

Tomme de Camargue see *Camargue*

Tomme de Champsaur

Soft goats' milk cheese from Dauphiné.

Tomme de Combovin 🝕 🝕 45% ⊝ 290g (7oz) ◐

Fairly mild cheese from Dauphiné ripened for a month. It has a blue-grey rind and a smooth white paste.

Tomme de Crest

One of the many soft goats' milk *tommes* made in Dauphiné. Similar to Tomme de Combovin.

Tomme au Fenouil

A Tomme de Savoie flavoured with fennel.

Tomme Fraîche

An unripened or partly ripened Cantal or Laguiole. Used a lot in local Auvergne cuisine. Also called Tomme d'Aligot.

Tomme au Marc ☒ 🝕 20–40% ⊝ 1.5–2kg (3–4lb) ◐

Not to be confused with the ubiquitous Tomme au Raisin, which is the processed version of this cheese. The authentic Tomme au Marc is an unpasteurized, pressed cheese made from partly skimmed milk. It is ripened for a total of six months partly in vats of fermented grape marc. Has an overpowering flavour with a smell to match.

Tomme de Mont Ventoux see *Cachat*

Tomme au Raisin see *Fondu au Raisin, Tomme au Marc*

Tomme de Savoie ★
Generic term for the countless semi-hard, pressed cows' milk cheeses made in Savoie from whole or partly skimmed milk by farms, *fruitières* and creameries. They are firm, smooth cheeses with a yellowy paste and a dry, hard, powdery rind varying in colour from greyish-white to pinky brown. The flavour is usually fairly mild and nutty and the fat content may be between 20 to 40 per cent.

Toupin   45%   6kg (13lb)
Pressed cooked cheese from Savoie, ripened for four to eight months. Resilient greyish rind; full-flavoured golden paste.

Trébèche, Trois Cornes see *Sableau*

Trouville
A type of rare, expensive farmhouse Pont l'Evêque.

Troyen Cendré see *Barberey*

Vachard   45%   1.5kg (3lb)
Cheese similar to Saint-Nectaire made on farms in Puy-de-Dôme. Tangy with a smooth grey crust.

Vacherin d'Abondance see *Abondance*

Vacherin des Beauges ★   45%   2kg (4lb)
Soft washed-rind cheese made in Savoie in autumn and winter. An old type suited to small farmhouse production. Ripened for three months, it has a pale pinkish-brown crust and a delicate, lightly spicy flavour. Bound with a strip of spruce bark and boxed. Also called Vacherin d'Aillons.

Vacherin Mont-d'Or ★   45%   2–3.5kg (4–8lb)
A superb cheese made in Franche Comté, similar to Vacherin des Beauges. The larger cheeses are generally superior to the smaller ones. Cheese experts recommend removing the whole rind and scooping out the paste of a ripe Vacherin with a spoon. Also made in Switzerland.

Valençay ★   45% 250g (9oz)
The *fermier* type is made in Berry from the end of spring until autumn. A flattened pyramid shape with a deep blue-grey surface covered with wood ash. Ripened for about five weeks, the paste is smooth and white with a delicate, by no means overpowering, goaty flavour. The commercial version, Valençay Laitier, is made all year round using frozen curds or powdered milk out of season. Ripened for a shorter time and coarser and stronger than the farmhouse type.

Venaco
Salty ewes' or goats' milk Corsican cheese, Square with wickerwork impressions on the surface, it has a greyish, coarse paste and is ripened for three to four months.

Vendôme Bleu   50%   200g (7oz)
From the Loire valley, a pleasant fruity flavoured cheese similar to Coulommiers but with a natural light blue-white rind. Ripened for about a month. Vendôme Cendré is the same

cheese ripened in the ashes of vine stems, but drier and stronger than Vendôme Bleu. Both are very rare.

Ventoux see *Cachat*

Vermenton
Rare, small, cone-shaped goat cheese from Burgundy.

Vieux Lille see *Gris de Lille*
Ville-Saint-Jacques see *Brie de Montereau*

Key words

Abbaye abbey. Denotes a monastery-made cheese, almost always using traditional methods and unpasteurized milk. See name of abbey in listing
Affiné ripened, cured, aged, as opposed to fresh
Affineur specialist cheese store where cheeses from various farms are taken for ripening
Appellation d'origine label of origin carried by cheeses conforming to legally defined conditions as to type and origin of milk, area of manufacture, production methods, physical characteristics. Guarantee of authenticity, but not necessarily of quality
Bleu see main listing
Bondon see main listing
Brebis ewe, ewes' milk cheese
Brique brick(-shaped)
Buron small mountain chalet where cheese is made by traditional methods
Carré square(-shaped)
Cendré see main listing
Chèvre see main listing
Cœur heart(-shaped)
Crème cream. *Crème de* . . . on labels indicates a processed cheese where the named cheese is the basic ingredient
Cru see *Lait cru*
Double-crème minimum fat content of 60 per cent
Extra-gras extra fat. Fat content of 45 to 60 per cent
Fermier farmhouse-made from unpasteurized milk; ripened on the farm or at an *affineur*
Feuille leaf; ripened or wrapped in leaves
Foin hay; ripened in hay
Fourme word denoting cheese, particularly that mountain-made in the Auvergne

Fondu see *Fromage Fondu* in main listing
Frais, fraîche unripened
Fromage cheese
Fromage Fort see main listing
Fruitières small co-operative dairies using milk of local farms, particularly in Savoie, Franche Comté and remote mountain areas
Gras fat. Fat content between 40 and 45 per cent
Haute montagne high mountain; cheeses so labelled are always better than the same cheese made in the valley since milk from summer pastures is used
Lait cru particular 'growth' of milk, from a specifically defined locality, with all its idiosyncrasies intact
Laitier creamery-made from pasteurized milk
Maigre low fat; less than 20 per cent
Mi-chèvre see *Chèvre* in main listing
Non pasteurisé unpasteurized
Pasteurisé pasteurized
Pavé slab(-shaped)
Persillé parsleyed; refers mostly to blue-veined cheeses made from ewes' or goats' milk or one of the two mixed with cows' milk
Pur chèvre see *Chèvre* in main listing
Tome, Tomme denotes cheeses, mainly from Dauphiné and Savoie
Trappiste monastery-made cheese. See *Abbaye*
Triple-crème triple cream. Minimum fat content of 75 per cent
Vache cow; its derivatives Vachard, Vacherin, Vacherol, etc., all denote cows' milk cheese

Germany

West Germany is one of the leading dairying nations, trailing only France, the United States and the USSR in terms of cheese production. Germans are inordinately fond of cheese, a fact which was noted centuries ago by Julius Caesar himself and is confirmed by modern marketing surveys. Even so, German cheeses have a limited international reputation. Most of them are scarcely known outside Germany and many Germans are themselves hard put to name more than three or four genuinely indigenous varieties. One of the reasons for the paradox is that a considerable proportion of the huge domestic production is taken up with foreign cheese types, and West German dairymen seem to be more interested in perfecting these cheeses and developing new varieties than they are in promoting their own national cheeses. Another reason is that the most important indigenous cheese is Quark, a fresh curd cheese which, until the advent of modern refrigerated transport, could not be successfully exported. Of the ripened types, the various kinds of Sauermilchkäse are generally so strong and pungent as to require a degree of acclimatization that most consumers are unprepared to concede to new and untried foodstuffs. In fact, with one or two exceptions, German cheeses tend to be either rather bland or rather strong.

Cheese is made all over Germany (almost entirely from cows' milk; there are few notable ewes' or goats' milk cheeses), but the most important area—the Normandy of Germany—is the Allgäu, where the Alps straddle the Swiss–German border. The word Allgäuer on a cheese label is a reliable guarantee of a quality product. As one might expect, quality control in cheesemaking is highly developed: German regulations and strictures on labelling are among the most detailed and precise in the world. There are no fewer than eight official categories of fat content:

Mager	less than 10%	low fat
Viertelfettstufe	10–20%	quarter fat
Halbfettstufe	20–30%	half fat
Dreiviertelfettstufe	30–40%	three-quarter fat
Fettstufe	40–45%	fat
Vollfettstufe	45–60%	full fat
Rahmstufe	50–60%	cream
Doppelrahmstufe	60–85%	double cream

Abertamerkäse see *Schafmilchkäse*
Alpenkäse see *Bergkäse*
Alte Kuhkäse see *Handkäse*

Ansgar
A milder sweeter version of Tilsit.

Backsteiner ☆ ◎ 38% ▭ 200g (7oz) ◖
'Brick' cheese; a washed-rind, surface-ripened, Limburger-type cheese made from partly skimmed milk.

Bauernhandkäse see *Handkäse*

Bavaria Blu   70%   1kg (2lb)
A recently invented hybrid cheese with a pale creamy paste showing splodges rather than veins of blue mould. It also has the white rind flora characteristic of Camembert types. Made from pasteurized cows' milk with additional cream.

Bergkäse   45%   50kg (110lb)
'Mountain cheese'; a hard-pressed cooked cheese with small round eyes, similar to Emmental but smaller in size, with a darker rind and a stronger, more aromatic flavour. Made in the Allgäu. Also called Alpenkäse.

Berliner Kuhkäse see *Handkäse*

Bianco   55%   4kg (9lb)
Trade name (from Italian, meaning 'white') for a pale, mild creamy cheese, with lots of small holes, similar to Tilsit.

Biarom   45%   1kg (2lb)
Trade name for a Bavarian cheese similar to Danish Esrom.

Bierkäse see *Weisslackerkäse*

Biestkäse
Freshly made from beestings. Also called Kolostrumkäse.

69

Bodenfelder see *Handkäse*

Bruder Basil 🌿 ➤ 45% ▱ 1kg (2lb) **6**
Smooth, firm, yellow cheese with a dark mahogany-coloured
rind, made in Bavaria. Creamy with a pleasantly smoky
flavour, it is a superior version of the Bavarian smoked
processed cheese one finds almost everywhere. There is also a
variation flavoured with chopped ham.

Butterkäse 🌿 ➤➤ 50% **€**
A smooth, bland and, as the name suggests, buttery cheese
made all over the country. The paste is a clear, pale yellow, with
or without irregular holes, and the rind is golden to reddish in
colour. It comes either in a loaf or in a wheel shape weighing 2kg
(4lb) and 1kg (2lb) respectively. It is extremely delicate,
odourless and quite inoffensive. Also called Damenkäse (ladies'
cheese).

Buttermilchquark
Fresh lactic-curd cheese made with a mixture of buttermilk and
skimmed milk.

Caramkäse
Smooth, bland, elastic cheese, occasionally smoked.

Damenkäse see *Butterkäse*
Doppelrahmfrischkäse see *Rahmfrischkäse*

Edelpilzkäse ★ 🌿 ➤➤ 45% 2–5kg (4–11lb) **6**
A fine blue-veined cheese with a pale ivory paste and very dark
veins travelling vertically through the cheese. It has a strong
fruity flavour. An excellent dessert cheese. The name, ap-
propriately, means 'glorious mould cheese' and it is sometimes
marketed outside Germany as 'German Blue'. It can be drum-
or loaf-shaped.

Edelschimmelkäse
A term which refers to cheeses that have blue veins or white rind
flora or both.

Emmental 🌿 ➤ 45% ▱ 40–90kg (88–198lb) **6**
Although Emmental is definitely Swiss, Allgäuer Emmental
has been made in Germany for centuries. Made from unpasteurized cows' milk, at its best when between six and eight
months old. See *Switzerland (Emmental)*

Friesischer Schafkäse, see *Schafmilchkäse*

Frischkäse
Generic term for fresh unripened cheeses made from pas-
teurized milk and coagulated with or without rennet. See
Quark, Rahmfrischkäse, Schichtkäse

Frühstückskäse 🌿 ➤➤ 10% 100–160g (3½–6oz) **€**
'Breakfast cheese'. Cheese is an important ingredient of the
German breakfast, especially the *Zweites Frühstück*, the 'second
breakfast' taken mid-morning, which fills in the gaps left by the
first one. This cheese is a small version of the Limburger type
made from whole or partly skimmed milk and eaten either fresh
or after a short ripening period, when the surface becomes
smeared with coryne moulds.

Gaiskäsle (Gaiskäsli) 🌙 50% 🧀 100g (3½oz) 🅾

A rare cheese made in the Allgäu from a mixture of unpasteurized goats' and pasteurized cows' milk. It is an unpressed surface-ripened cheese in two variations: one a brownish washed-rind cheese with a coryne smear, the other milder with white rind flora. The ripening period is between two and three weeks.

Geheimratskäse 🌡 🌙 40–60% 0.5kg (18oz) 🅱

Small loaf- or wheel-shaped Edam-type cheese with a few small round holes in the pale close-textured paste. Coated in wax.

Geräuchter— smoked.
Bayrischer— Bavarian.
Schnittkäse— sliceable cheese

Fett. i. Tr.— fat content
Naturgereift— naturally ripened

Handkäse ★

Generic term for small, traditionally hand-moulded cheeses made from sour milk curds, descendants of the earliest, most primitive form of cheesemaking. They come in a wide range of shapes—bars, rolls, discs, squares—and vary in flavour from delicate to powerfully sharp. Many are additionally flavoured with herbs or spices. They can have smooth rinds or be covered in mould smears and pure white, buff or yellowy orange in colour. All of them are low in fat and high in protein. The innumerable variations are often found under specific (usually regional) designations including Harzer, Mainzer, Rheinischer, Odenwalder, Bauernhandkäse, Bodenfelder, Berliner Kuhkäse, Stangenkäse, Spitzkäse, Korbkäse and Alte Kuhkäse. In Hesse eaten with 'Musik', an onion and vinegar garnish, and in the Harz mountains with goose dripping.

Hartkäse

Generic term for hard cheeses such as Emmental.

Harzer see *Handkäse*

Hauskäse

A small cheese similar to Limburger.

Holsteiner Magerkäse

Made in Schleswig Holstein from skimmed milk sometimes mixed with buttermilk. Also called Lederkäse ('leather cheese', a pretty accurate description).

Holsteinermarschkäse see *Wilstermarschkäse*
Hopfenkäse see *Nieheimer Hopfenkäse*

Klosterkäse

A soft surface-ripened cows' milk cheese similar to Limburger.

Kolostrumkäse see *Biestkäse*

Korbkäse see *Handkäse*

Kräuterkäse
Generic term for cheeses flavoured with herbs.

Kühbacher
Soft cheese made near Munich from a mixture of whole and
partly skimmed milk.

Kümmelkäse
A small, soft, washed-rind, low-fat cheese made from partly
skimmed cows' milk and flavoured with caraway seeds

Labfrischkäse, Labquark
Fresh curd cheese coagulated with rennet (from *Lab*, rennet).
Sometimes used as the basis for Sauermilchkäse. See *Quark*

Lederkäse see *Holsteiner Magerkäse*

Limburger ★ ☆ ☾ 20–50% ▢ 200g–1kg (7oz–2lb) 🌢
Strictly speaking, of Belgian origin, but adopted by Allgäuer
dairymen in the 19th century. A washed-rind, surface-ripened
cheese with a slightly moist, typically reddish-brown skin and a
creamy rich yellow paste. After moulding and draining, the
cheeses are salted in brine for seven to 24 hours depending on the
size of the cheese and then washed at intervals with coryne
bacteria. After about a month the yellowy mould begins to
develop on the surface, becoming darker and firmer during a
further ripening period of eight weeks or so. Despite the many
jokes surrounding the notorious ferocity of Limburger it should
not, at least in appearance, be in the least menacing. As far as
flavour goes, its decidedly aromatic bark is considerably worse
than its bite. If the paste is runny or the rind slimy it means that
the cheese is overripe and well past its best. It is available in
various grades according to fat content. The lower the fat the
firmer the cheese.

Mainauerkäse ☆ ☾ 40–60% ▭ 1.5kg (3lb) 🌢
A Münster type named after an island in Lake Constance.

Mainzer see *Handkäse*
Marschkäse see *Wilstermarschkäse*

Münster ☆ ☾ 45% ▭ 1kg (2lb) 🌢
Another 'borrowed' cheese, this time from Alsace. Munster
(without an umlaut) is French; Münster (with an umlaut) is
German. The cheese has a smooth, softish, yellow paste with a
thin brown skin and a mildly piquant flavour.

Nieheimer Hopfenkäse
Similar but not identical to Hopfenkäse. Both are made from
sour milk curds partially ripened then broken up, remoulded,
and allowed to ripen for a further period packed in boxes
between layers of hops. In both, the curds are mixed with
caraway seeds, but the Hopfenkäse curds, after the initial
ripening, are mixed with fresh curds whereas for Nieheimer
Hopfenkäse they are mixed with full milk or, occasionally, beer
before being remoulded by hand into small cakes. Dry cheese
good for grating.

Odenwalder see *Handkäse*

Quark ★

A fresh unripened curd cheese that can be made from skimmed milk, whole milk, buttermilk or any of these mixed with added cream. The fat content varies from 10 to 60 per cent. Quark accounts for almost half the German cheese production and is eaten in vast quantities and in innumerable ways. One way and another the Germans each manage to eat about 5kg (11lb) per annum, nearly half their total consumption of all types of cheese. The name, incidentally, simply means 'curds'. See *Buttermilchquark*, *Labquark*, *Speisequark*

Radolfzeller Rahmkäse

Surface-ripened cheese similar to Mainauer, drained on straw mats, dry salted and ripened for about a month.

Rahmfrischkäse

Fresh unripened cream cheese usually sold in small foil-wrapped cubes. Made by adding more cream to Speisequark. For Doppelrahmfrischkäse (double-cream cheese) even more cream is added, bringing the fat content up to 60 per cent.

Räucherkäse

Generic term for smoked cheese which, in most cases, does not mean that the cheese has been literally smoked but that artificial 'smoky' flavouring has been added to the milk.

Rheinischer see *Handkäse*

Romadur

Similar to Limburger but softer and milder. Also a washed-rind, surface-ripened cheese with a yellowish-brown skin and a rich golden paste which has a scattering of irregular holes. Made either from whole or partly skimmed milk and in various grades of fat content. The brining and ripening periods are shorter than those for Limburger, about four hours and two weeks respectively, and the flavour and aroma are consequently less assertive. It should be kept quite cool and not allowed to become overripe. Like Limburger, it originated in Belgium, where a similar cheese is known as Remoudou.

Rotschmierkäse

Generic term for cheeses like Limburger, Romadur and Münster which have reddish skins produced by the action of coryne bacteria on the surface of the cheese during ripening.

Sauermilchkäse

Generic term for cheeses made from sour milk curds, in other words from milk coagulated with a lactic acid starter rather than rennet. Includes all the Handkäse types.

Schafmilchkäse

Generic term for ewes' milk cheese. Only Schnittkäse can officially be made from ewes' milk in Germany. Two good cheeses are Abertamerkäse and Friesischer Schafkäse.

Schichtkäse

A fresh unripened curd cheese combining layers (hence the name 'layer cheese') of skimmed milk and whole milk curds.

Schimmelkäse

Sauermilchkäse treated with moulds.

Schnittkäse

'Sliceable cheese', one of the official categories of cheese covering semi-hard varieties like Tilsit and Trappistenkäse.

Speisequark

Quark made from skimmed milk curds mixed with some of the skimmed fats, graded according to the proportion of fat replaced.

Spitzkäse

'Sharp cheese'; a roll- or bar-shaped Sauermilchkäse made from skimmed milk curds mixed with caraway seeds. It has a clear buff-coloured surface smear and is fairly piquant.

Stangenkäse

'Bar cheese', actually shaped like a thin sausage; a type of Sauermilchkäse, tangy and flavoured with caraway seeds.

Tilsit(er) ★   30–50%

Named after the town of Tilsit (now Soviet Sovetsk), where it was first made by Dutch immigrants in the mid 19th century. It has a lovely buttery yellow paste with many small elliptical holes. The consistency is springy and elastic yet rather moist and creamy and the flavour is mild and delicate with spicy undertones. Made from whole or skimmed milk and the skimmed milk type is sometimes flavoured with caraway seeds. The curds are lightly scalded in the whey before being moulded in stainless steel hoops and, in some places, very lightly pressed. The initial ripening period lasts for about a month, during which time the cheeses are regularly washed with brine. Afterwards they are stored for about five months before being sold. The traditional shape for Tilsit is a large wheel but the loaf shape tailored to the demands of slicing machines is becoming increasingly common.

Trappistenkäse

A mild yellow cheese full of tiny holes and shaped like a huge fat sausage or a rectangular block. Made in southern and central Germany.

Weichkäse

Generic term for soft surface-ripened cheeses.

Weinkäse ★   30–50%   75g (2½oz)

A small, round, creamy, mild cheese whose name derives from its particular affinity with wine. Has a superb glossy paste and a thin, smooth, pinkish skin.

Weisslackerkäse

    40–50%   600g–2kg (21oz–4lb)

The shiny white surface of this Bavarian cuboid cheese is presumably responsible for the name, which means 'white lacquer'. It is a surface-ripened cheese, developed about 100 years ago, and is extremely pungent with a powerfully piquant flavour, becoming even more pronounced with age. Made from a mixture of skimmed evening and whole morning milk, it is salted, dry or in brine, for two to three days before being placed in conditions of high humidity for a few more days, the cheeses just touching, for the surface flora to develop. They are then separated and ripened for up to seven months. Also called Weisslacker Bierkäse.

Wilstermarschkäse 🥛 ≫ 45–50% ▭ 1.5–6kg (3–13lb) 🌙
An ivory-coloured slightly sour-tasting cheese from Wilster in Schleswig Holstein and, like Tilsit, said to have been invented by Dutch immigrants. It can be made from whole or partly skimmed milk and is ripened for about four weeks. Also called Holsteinermarschkäse, Marschkäse.

Ziegenkäse
Generic term for goats' milk cheese.

GERMAN DEMOCRATIC REPUBLIC

East German cheeses hold little interest for the rest of the world. There are few indigenous types and even these are not exported. There are many similarities with West German tastes, such as a fondness for Quark, Sauermilchkäse and Handkäse. Foreign types, notably Chester and Cheddar, are made, largely for the manufacture of processed cheeses.

Altenburger Ziegenkäse ★ ≫ 20–45% ⊖ 250g (9oz) ●
Made in Thuringia from a mixture of unpasteurized cows' and goats' milk. A rare connoisseur's cheese with a rich yellow paste punctuated with a few irregular eyes and flavoured with caraway seeds. Very strong-tasting and aromatic. Treated with both *Penicillium camemberti* and coryne bacteria during the ripening period, it is a temperamental cheese and one that is very difficult to make successfully.

Mecklenburger Magerkäse 🥛 ≫ ⊖ 🌙
Hard-pressed, skimmed milk cheese, coloured with saffron.

Steinbuscherkäse ★ 🥛 ≫ 30–50% 200–700g (7–25oz) 🌙
A yellowy brown cube-shaped washed-rind cheese with a smooth, firm, pale straw-coloured paste, mildly piquant in flavour and fairly strong smelling. First produced in the mid 19th century in Steinbusch (now Choszczno, in Poland). Also made in West Germany. Ripened for between two and three months.

Steppenkäse 🥛 ≫ 35% ⊖ 7–12kg (15–26lb) 🌙
Rich buttery greyish-yellow cheese with a pronounced full-bodied flavour. Originally made in the USSR by German immigrants from whole milk coloured with annatto and cured in cool humid conditions for about three months.

Tieflanderkäse
A hard-cooked cheese with eyes, similar to Emmental.

Tollenser
East German name for Tilsit. See *Federal Republic*

Key words	
Alt old, mature	**Reif** mature, ripe
Frisch fresh, young	**Schaf** sheep
Hart hard	**Scharf** strong
Jung young	**Schmelzkäse**
Käse cheese	processed cheese
Kuh cow	**Weich** soft
Rahm cream	**Ziege** goat

Greece and Cyprus

The cradle of Western civilization is, in some ways, a bleak and barren land. 'Poverty,' said Herodotus, 'has lived in Greece since ancient times.' The image of Arcadia with its lush groves peopled by gods and heroes was perhaps a necessary counterpoint to the harsh realities of everyday life. In that unpromising terrain only the most resilient of plant and animal life could survive: the hardy olive and the equally tenacious sheep. Meat always was, and still is, something of a luxury in Greece, so that cheese has provided a major source of protein for thousands of years in an otherwise often frugal diet. This is reflected in Greek mythology and folklore: the shepherd is a recurrent, even romantic figure in many stories. The gargantuan appetite of Polyphemus (himself a cheesemaker) almost matches the present-day consumption of cheese in Greece, which is one of the highest per head in the world. The domestic demand for cheese is so great that its export has been banned for many years. The small amounts of Haloumi and Kefalotiri that find their way into foreign markets come from Cyprus; the Feta may be German, Bulgarian, Australian, American or Danish. Another result of the shortage is that many of the cheeses traditionally made with ewes' milk (such as Feta, the cheese made by Polyphemus) are now being made with cows' milk, or at least a mixture of the two.

Anari ('Αναρί)   🗲 ➋ 20% 🧀 ▢

Mizithra made in Cyprus, where it is eaten fresh with sugar, honey and candied fruit or dried and used for grating.

Anthotiri ('Ανθοτύρι)   🗲 ➋ 35% ▢

A fresh, white, unripened cheese made in Crete. The name means 'flowery cheese'; it is in fact usually flavoured with herbs or sweetened with honey.

Fet(t)a (Φέτ(τ)α) ★   🗲 50% ◇ 🧀 🜂

Sharp, salty, white cheese, either firm and crumbly or hard. The American, Australian, German, Italian and Danish versions are made from pasteurized cows' milk while the original Greek Feta (like the Bulgarian) is still made mostly from ewes' milk, although it is currently available only in Greece because of the export ban. Ewes' milk Feta has a fat content between five and ten per cent higher than the cows' milk cheese. It has been made in Greece by more or less the same method for thousands of years. Fresh milk is curdled by lactic fermentation and the curds and whey are then reheated together causing the remaining fats and proteins in the whey to flocculate. The curds are scooped into cloths or ladled into moulds to drain and then turned and lightly pressed at regular intervals. When sufficiently firm they are cut into blocks and salted in brine for varying amounts of time. The longer the salting, the harder the cheese becomes. The saltier kinds are best soaked in a little milk or lukewarm water to temper the flavour.

Feta is eaten in vast quantities in Greece (so much so that it also has to be imported, mostly from Denmark). It can be eaten with crusty bread for breakfast or with olives and sliced raw tomatoes for a light lunch. It is crumbled or cubed into the typical Greek mixed salads and used in stuffings for aubergines, peppers and vineleaves. It may be crumbled on to stews or used to fill deliciously light Greek flaky pastries, such as *tiropitta* (tiny cheese puffs). In Greece, Feta is sold floating in a brine bath, but elsewhere it is generally found in vacuum packs. See *Bulgaria (Feta)*

Only Achaean cattle graze vigorous and strong
On abundant fields in Thessaly beneath an ageless,
  watching sun
They eat green grass and celery, leaves of the poplar tree,
  they drink clear water in the troughs
They smell the sweat of the earth and then fall heavily
  to sleep in the shade of the willow tree.

Nikos Gatsos from AMORGOS

Galotiri (Γαλοτύρι)

A 'home-made' cross between Feta and Mizithra. Fresh ewes' milk is allowed to ripen for an hour or so and then boiled to separate the curds and whey. The curds are scooped out, salted, stirred from time to time during the following few days and then placed in animal skins to drain. The next day's milking will be treated in the same way and added to the first batch. Eaten after three months.

Graviera (Γραβιέρα)   50%   20–40kg (44–88lb)

The second most popular cheese in Greece after Feta, this Greek version of Gruyère is yellowish in colour, with holes and an exceptionally hard rind. It is a rich, creamy cheese, eaten as an hors d'oeuvre, after a meal or even during the main course, sliced as a side dish. The Cretan version, made with ewes' milk, is much sought after.

Haloumi (Χαλούμι) ★   40%

Creamy white cheese with a somewhat fibrous texture, generally less salty than Feta even though it is also soaked in brine during processing. Firmer than Feta and less brittle, it can be sliced but not crumbled. In Cyprus the cheese is dipped in hot water, kneaded with chopped mint, rolled out like pastry and cut into bars. It is either eaten soon after making or ripened for about a month. About ten per cent of the Haloumi produced is made with cows' milk and this must be eaten within a month or it becomes impossibly hard. The ewes' milk type is used a great deal in cooking. It can be grated on top of *moussaka*, sliced in salads, or dipped into hot water and pulled out in strings to be eaten as a snack. Very often it is sliced and fried in oil and eaten for breakfast with fried eggs and raw tomatoes. It should be washed in lukewarm water or milk before using.

Kaseri (Κασέρι)   40%   9kg (20lb)

Hard-pressed, strong white cheese with a scattering of tiny holes, which provides an example of a happy invention mothered by necessity. In thrifty rural economies (often near or just above subsistence level), nothing can be wasted; and yet cheesemaking, especially before the days of scientific agriculture, was often a hit or miss affair. So much could go wrong, and frequently did. However, rather than consign unsuccessful cheeses to the dustbin, in Greece they make them into Kaseri. The cheeses are dipped in hot water (like Italian *pasta filata*), then kneaded and shaped or moulded into large wheels. In fact, Kaseri is very similar to Provolone Dolce in texture and the

77

Greeks prefer it to Mozzarella on pizza. It is also eaten sliced as a table cheese, or can be dipped in flour and fried in oil.

Kefalograviera (Κεφαλογραβιέρα) 40%

A combination of Kefalotiri and Graviera eaten almost exclusively as a table cheese. The taste is nearer to Graviera but a little more salty, and the cheese is usually slightly smaller, although all these cheeses do tend to vary in size. Generally speaking, the larger the whole cheese, the better the flavour.

Kefalotiri (Κεφαλοτύρι) 40%

Close-textured, slightly oily cheese, pale biscuit-coloured with a thin, hard rind and a pronounced ewes' milk tang. Somewhat harder than Kaseri, it is used mainly in cooking. The name 'head cheese' comes from its supposed resemblance to a Greek hat. Most of the Kefalotiri found outside Greece is Kefalograviera, since the original is too strong for foreign tastes.

We did not find [Polyphemus] at home, for he was herding fat sheep in the field. With great astonishment we looked at everything. There were racks heavy laden with cheeses . . . The casks were overflowing with whey.

Homer THE ODYSSEY

Kopanisti (Κοπανιστή)

A veined cheese from the Aegean Islands made from cows' or ewes' milk. The fresh curds are roughly cut, put into cloths to drain for a few hours, then hand moulded into balls and left to dry. After a while the surface of the cheese becomes covered with mould, and this is worked back into the cheese with a quantity of salt. The cheeses are then left to ripen for a couple of months until they become soft, creamy and salty. Some of the best come from the island of Mykonos.

Manouri (Μανούρι)

Fresh, whole ewes' milk cheese from Crete. It is white and creamy and slightly firmer than Mizithra, shaped into ovals and waxed or packaged in foil. Eaten with honey as a dessert.

Mizithra (Μυζήθρα) 20%

Whey cheese made from the by-products of Feta and Kefalotiri. Whole fresh ewes' or cows' milk is sometimes added to make it richer. Similar to Italian Ricotta, it is used in cooking in much the same way and is also eaten fresh, sometimes while still warm. It is occasionally preserved in salt and can also be dried and used for grating. See *Anari*

Teleme (Τελεμέ)

Feta cheese from northern Greece.

Key words

Agelada (Ἀγελάδα) cow	**Palio (Παληό)** mature
Elafro (Ἐλαφρό) mild	**Pikantiko (Πικάντικο)** piquant
Fresco (Φρέσκο) fresh	**Provatina (Προβατίνα)** ewe
Katsika (Κατσίκα) goat	**Skliro (Σκληρό)** hard
Malako (Μαλακό) soft	**Tiri (Τυρί)** cheese

HUNGARY see *Eastern Europe*,
ICELAND see *Scandinavia*. INDIA see *Asia*. IRAQ see *Middle East*.

Israel

The modern Israeli dairy industry is highly mechanized and efficient, dominated by Tnuva, a huge co-operative controlling over 80 per cent of milk produced. All cheese is made from pasteurized milk, mainly copying European types.

Atzmon
Soft, buttery, cows' milk cheese similar to Italian Bel Paese.

Bashan
Smoked sausage-shaped cheese with a shiny red rind. Made from mixed ewes' and goats' milk. Fairly piquant.

Duberki
Drained yoghurt shaped into balls. Dried or steeped in oil.

Ein-Gedi
Foil-wrapped Camembert-type made from cows' milk.

Emek
Hard, full-fat, loaf-shaped cows' milk cheese with a red rind.

Gad
From G'vina Danit, meaning 'Danish cheese'. Springy yellow loaf with scattered small holes. Modelled on Danish Danbo.

Galil
Fairly strong ewes' milk green-veined Roquefort type.

Gewina Zfatit
Fresh, white, salty ewes' milk cheese. Lightly pressed in round baskets that leave a surface impression. Cows' and/or goats' milk may be added. Sometimes ripened until dry and hard.

Gilboa
Semi-hard, mild cows' milk loaf similar to Edam.

Gilead
Full-fat, drum-shaped ewes' milk *pasta filata* cheese.

Golan
Hard ewes' milk *pasta filata* cheese similar to Italian Provolone.

Jizrael
Hard, pressed cooked cheese with large holes like Emmental.

Kol-Bee
Loaf-shaped imitation Gouda made from cows' milk.

Tal Ha'Emek
Pasteurized copy of Emmental.

Thou shalt not seethe a kid in its mother's milk. Exodus 23.19. Jewish dietary laws forbid the mixing of milk, and therefore all dairy products, with meat. This means that animal rennet cannot be used in cheesemaking. Vegetable rennets are used instead to manufacture kosher versions of many cheese types, also acceptable to most vegetarians and widely exported from Israel.

The Ancient Romans considered the idea of drinking fresh milk rather nauseating. They preferred to consume milk in the form of cheese and even in those days there was an astonishing variety. They could choose from fresh, smoked or dried cheeses, cheeses coagulated with fig juice or flavoured with marjoram, mint and coriander, a Grana-type cheese called Lunar, ewes' milk cheeses and goats' cheeses from Liguria. Foreign cheeses were imported as well, such as English Cheshire, a ewes' milk cheese called Cythnos from Greece and two French cheeses, one almost certainly Roquefort and the other Cantal. Cheeses were exported throughout the Empire together with the Romans' cheesemaking expertise and although much of this knowledge was lost during the Dark Ages, some survived in isolated communities all over Europe to form the basis of the extraordinarily wide range available nowadays.

Italians are just as enthusiastic about cheese today. They use it a great deal in cooking, as well as eating it at the end of meals (before, rather than after, the dessert). The range of Italian cheese types is quite magnificent and each cheese is superb of its kind. Quite apart from native Italian inventiveness, the geography of the country lends itself to a wide variety of cheeses, stretching as it does from the sweet alpine pastures down the mountainous leg of Italy almost as far as Africa. Cows and sheep have flourished in different parts of the country for centuries in well-nigh perfect conditions. Even the swamps of central and southern Italy, barren in every other way, proved ideal for the water buffalo whose milk adds an unusual element to the cheese range.

There are approximately twice as many sheep as cows in Italy, mainly in the centre and south; their numbers decrease towards the north. The distribution of cows is almost exactly reversed and this pattern is closely reflected in the traditional areas associated with the two types of cheese. Lombardy,

Piedmont and the Po valley (in the north) are renowned for
cows' milk types. Tuscany, Lazio, Sardinia, Campania,
Puglia, Sicily and the whole of central and southern Italy
produce marvellous ewes' milk cheeses, which become more
piccante the farther south one goes. This is admittedly an
oversimplified view of Italian cheesemaking, because when
the focus shifts to individual cheeses on a local level there is
a bewildering plethora of idiosyncratic variations and
confusing designations to wade through. The same cheese
may be sold under several different names and one name
may be applied to many cheeses which are often totally
different in character. Until you are able to do as the
Italians do, and rely on the evidence of your eyes, nose and
tastebuds to ascertain what you are buying, the following
listing will provide, at best, an imperfect guide.

Aostin

Buttery, sweet-tasting cows' milk cheese made in spring on
mountain farms in Aosta.

Asiago

30% 9–13kg (20–29lb)

Originally a ewes' milk cheese from the wild and rocky pine-
clad plateau of Asiago in the foothills of the Dolomites, this
cheese is now made from cows' milk throughout the province of
Vicenza. Skimmed evening milk is added to whole morning
milk. After coagulation the curds are scalded, pressed and
ripened, producing a very firm cheese with a granular, yellowy
buff paste with small, evenly scattered holes and a smooth,
hard, golden rind. The ripening period varies between two and
six months for a pleasantly sharp table cheese (Asiago di taglio
or Asiago grasso di monte) to a year or more for an extra strong
grating cheese (Asiago da allievo).

Baccellone

Ewes' milk cheese similar to Ricotta Siciliana, made in and
around Livorno especially in spring. Eaten with fresh broad
beans (*baccelli*).

Bagozzo

Bland, whitish-yellow cows' milk cheese made in Brescia,
especially around Lake Iseo. Basically a simple country cheese,
its production is small-scale and erratic. Some cheeses are
allowed to mature to a more piquant flavour and firmer texture.
Also known as Bresciano and Grana Bagozzo.

Bel Paese

52% 2kg (4lb)

This sweet, buttery cheese, pale yellow with a smooth springy
texture and a shiny golden rind, is a spectacularly successful
20th century invention, created by Egidio Galbani in 1906 and
made in Melzo, Lombardy. It is an uncooked, pressed and
quick-ripening cheese. The name (meaning 'beautiful
country') derives from the book written by Abbot Antonio
Stoppani, a friend of the Galbani family. His portrait, imposed
on a map of Italy, appears on the foil wrapping in which the
cheese is sold. The American version depicts a map of the
western hemisphere. See *Italico*

Bitto

Originally from Friuli, now made throughout Lombardy on an
irregular basis, this simple rustic cheese is made from skimmed

cows' milk or a mixture of cows' and goats', or ewes' and goats' milk. It is a scalded, pressed, firm cheese with small eyes, ripened for a month or so for use as a table cheese or longer for grating. Similar to Fontina.

Bocconi Giganti
Meaning 'giant mouthfuls', small smoked Provolone-type cheeses.

Borelli
Small buffalo milk cheeses occasionally flavoured with cumin or caraway seeds.

One of the most successful factory-made cheeses in the world. A brand name that has become a widely imitated type.

Galbani alone can make Bel Paese in Italy. Made in other countries under licence

Bra
🏠 ⟩ 30% ⊖ 5kg (11lb) ▶

From Piedmont, a strong, white, salty cheese made at one time by nomadic herdsmen and now produced on an occasional basis from partly skimmed milk. The curds are shredded into minute pieces, moulded and pressed, then repeatedly broken up and pressed again so that the final texture is extremely dense and compact. The double salting, by immersing the cheeses in brine and rubbing salt into the surface, intensifies the flavour; not a cheese for faint hearts or sensitive palates.

Bresciano see *Bagozzo*
Brocotte see *Ricotta*

Burrini
🏠 ⟩ 45% 200–300g (7–10oz) 🧈

A speciality of southern Italy, Puglia and Calabria in particular. Small, pear-shaped, *pasta filata* cheeses, hand moulded around a pat of sweet butter, with a mild taste and a faint tang rather like Provolone dolce. They are ripened for a few weeks only and eaten with bread spread with the buttery heart of the cheese. For longer keeping, especially for export, the cheeses are dipped in wax. Also known as Butirri, Burielli and occasionally Provole.

Cacetti
🏠 ⟩ 44% 🧈

Small, pear-shaped, spun-curd cheeses. After moulding, the cheeses are dipped in wax and hung up by a loop of raffia attached at the narrow end to mature for about ten days.

Caciocavallo ★
🏠 ⟩ 44% 2–3kg (4–7lb) ● 🧈

Type of cheese prevalent throughout the eastern Mediterranean and the Balkans and known under a variety of similar names. Light straw-coloured and close-textured with, occasionally, a few holes scattered through the paste, and a smooth, thin, golden yellow or brownish rind. These spun-curd cheeses are moulded by hand into fat skittle shapes and ripened for three months or so for a table cheese (sweet and delicate) and longer for grating. The ripening method, whereby the cheeses are hung in pairs over poles as if on horseback (*a cavallo*) accounts for one theory as to the origin of the curious name. Another suggests that the cheese was originally made with mares' milk. If true, this would make Caciocavallo the oldest Italian cheese, dating back to the nomadic era when mares' milk was an occasional food (though whether there was ever a surplus that could be used in cheesemaking seems most unlikely). In any case, it was almost certainly known in Roman times. Columella in his classic treatise on agriculture *De Rustica* (AD 35–45) described precisely the method for making it.

Caciocavallo Siciliano   ● 42% ▽ 7–12kg (15–26½lb) ◗

Essentially the same as Caciocavallo except that goats' milk may be mixed with the cows' milk and the curds are pressed in oblong moulds rather than being shaped by hand. It is salted for about three weeks and then dipped in wax.

Cacio Fiore

A Caciotta made in winter from ewes' or goats' milk coagulated with vegetable rennet and tinted with saffron.

Caciotta ★   ● 42% ▱ 1–2kg (2–4lb) ◖

Deliciously creamy, softish small cheese ranging in colour from white to golden yellow and in flavour from sweet and mild to lightly piquant. The factory-made version is made from pasteurized cows' milk and tends to be rather bland. Otherwise, Caciotta can be made from any type of milk, since the term is less descriptive of a particular cheese type than an indication that this is a small cheese made from local milk by artisans and farmers in the traditional manner. These farmhouse versions show innumerable regional variations in flavour and shape. Some have smooth, firm, oiled rinds, others have the basket-work imprint typical of some Pecorinos. They are usually aged for about ten days. The best are said to be Caciotta di Urbino and Caciotta Toscana (traditionally eaten with fresh young broad beans). See *Bagozzo, Cacio Fiore, Chiavara, Fresa, Toscanello*

Canestrato   ◤ 45% ▱ 2kg (4lb) ● ◖

Traditionally a ewes' milk cheese from Sicily, pressed in a wicker mould (*canestro*) which leaves its imprint on the outside of the cheese. Made between October and June it has a dense, whitish-yellow paste with a few scattered holes. Also known as Incanestrato and sometimes as Pecorino Siciliano or Pecorino Canestrato (or Incanestrato) to distinguish it from the cows' milk version of the same cheese. When the feminine form of the word is used (Canestrata or Incanestrata) it denotes a hard, matured ewes' milk Ricotta made especially for grating.

Caprini

As the name suggests, (from *capra*, goat) these small delicate lactic-curd cheeses were once made with goats' milk. Goats' milk cheeses have however disappeared almost entirely in Italy and nowadays Caprini are produced almost exclusively from cows' milk. They are eaten fresh with sugar or with olive oil and seasoning.

Caprini di Montevecchia

Matured Caprini, distinguishable by a thin covering of brownish mould.

Caprino Romano see *Romano*

Casiddi
Small hard goats' or ewes' milk cheeses from Basilicata.

Casigliolo
Caciocavallo-type cheese made in Sicily. Also called Panedda and Pera di Vacca.

Casizzolu
A mild *pasta filata* cheese made in Sardinia, where it is often eaten toasted over an open fire.

Castelmagno
Blue-veined cows' milk cheese similar to Gorgonzola. Named after a mountain village near Dronero, Piedmont.

Casu Becciu, Casu Iscaldidu, Casu Marzu
Pungent crumbly cheeses made in spring from cows' or goats' milk in the Gallura region of Sardinia.

Certosa, Certosino see *Stracchino*

Chiavara
A Caciotta made from cows' milk near Genoa.

Ciccillo see *Provola*

Cotronese, Crotonese
Ewes' (or ewes' and goats') milk cheese made in small dairies near Crotone, Calabria. Sometimes flavoured with whole black peppercorns.

Crema Bel Paese
A processed cheese spread but surprisingly acceptable even though a little metallic in flavour. See *Bel Paese*

Cremini
Originally the name for small, full-fat, fresh cream cheeses but now applied to any mild cheese spread (usually processed).

Dolcelatte 🍴 🧀 50% 🧀 1–2kg (2–4lb) 🅐
Smooth, creamy, blue-veined cheese, deliciously mild and delicate (the name, a registered trade mark, means 'sweet milk'). It is a factory-made, more easily digestible version of Gorgonzola. Sometimes labelled Gorgonzola Dolcelatte.

Dolceverde
Factory-made cheese similar to Dolcelatte.

Emiliano 🍴 ➤ 32% 🧀 20–30kg (44–56lb) ● ℂ
Pale yellow Grana-type cheese from Emilia with a dark brownish-black oiled rind. Ripened between one and two years.

Fiore d'Alpe
A cows' milk cheese from Lodi, Lombardy, similar to Bel Paese.

Fior di Latte 🍴 🧀 45% ● 🅑
The official designation for Mozzarella made with cows' milk, meaning 'the cream of the milk'.

Fiore Sardo   ≫ 45%   🍥 3kg (7lb) 🧀 🅾

White, creamy cheese made from a mixture of whole ewes' and goats' milk by Sardinian shepherds. It is generally milder than a traditional Pecorino Sardo made entirely with ewes' milk. Also called Fioretto Sardo.

Foggiano

Type of Pecorino (the ewes' milk is sometimes mixed with cows' or goats' milk) from Foggia, in Puglia.

Fontal   🍥 ➌ 45%   🍥 6–20kg (13–44lb) 🧀 🅱

Cheese similar to Fontina which was, in fact, called Fontina until the Stresa Convention of 1951 protected the exclusive claims of the Val d'Aosta. It is produced on an industrial scale throughout Piedmont and Lombardy but unlike genuine Fontina it is made largely from pasteurized milk, and has fewer eyes and a slightly darker rind.

Fontina ★   🍥 ➌ 45%   🍥 8–18kg (18–40lb) 🧀 🅱

One of the best of the many excellent Italian cheeses, genuine Fontina comes only from the Val d'Aosta high up in the Alps near the borders with France and Switzerland. Made from whole unpasteurized milk of one milking, it is a pressed, cooked, medium-ripened cheese with a smooth, slightly elastic, straw-coloured paste that has sparse small round holes. The rind is an uneven light brown, thin and lightly oiled. Fontina has a delicate, nutty, almost honeyed flavour, somewhat like Swiss Gruyère but sweeter and more buttery. The best is made in mountain chalets between May and September when the herds pasture on the alpine meadows. In the winter months the milk is processed in small cheese factories in the valleys. Like Gruyère in *fondue*, Fontina is the most important ingredient in the Piedmontese version, *fonduta*, which boasts the additional speciality of white truffles.

Formaggelle

Small, soft cheeses made from ewes', goats' or cows' milk in the mountains of northern Italy, particularly around Brianza. Usually eaten fresh, but sometimes salted and kept longer.

Formaggini

Generic name for small cheeses. Usually refers to processed cheeses or cheese spreads but can sometimes denote small, locally made cheeses.

Fresa

A Caciotta—mild, sweet, almost sugary—made from cows' or goats' milk in Sardinia.

Friulana

An exceptionally piquant, hard, close-textured cheese made from cows' milk in the countryside around Venice.

Gorgonzola ★   🍥 ≫ 48%   🍥 6–12kg (13–26½lb) 🧀 🅰

Italy's principal blue-veined cheese has enjoyed a deservedly high international reputation for generations. Originally a winter-made cheese, a Stracchino, it has the mild creamy paste typical of that wonderfully fertile family of Lombardy cheeses. Its greenish-blue mould gives Gorgonzola the sharp, almost spicy flavour which contrasts so agreeably with the delicacy of the paste. The naturally formed rind is coarse and reddish-grey in colour with powdery patches. Many decidedly apocryphal tales have arisen to explain its origins well over 1,000 years ago. One that seems plausible tells how migrating herdsmen travelling south to winter pastures stopped over at the village of Gorgonzola near Milan and, embarrassed by the innkeepers' bills, paid in kind with freshly made cheeses. Having no use for this unexpected windfall, the innkeepers stored them in their cellars, which provided ideal conditions for natural mould formation. (The caves at Valsassina and Lodi were later to fulfil the same purpose.) With the typically Italian genius for improvisation in matters of food, the innkeepers served these 'mouldy' cheeses to their guests, apparently to their considerable satisfaction.

My favourite food, as a child, was cheese, and cheese had to be stolen; for authority did not think that large wedges of Gorgonzola was good for delicate, highly-strung little Gladys. I would rob the sideboard whenever I had a chance, of a hunk about the size of my fist, and carrying it away to the nursery or a quiet part of the garden, nibble it in solitude, and think beautiful thoughts of fairies and ladybirds, and how nice it was to be good.
G.B. Stern *The Child as Epicure* from THE EPICURE'S COMPANION

Nowadays Gorgonzola is still made in Lombardy, but all the year round and no longer at Gorgonzola itself. *Penicillium glaucum* is added to whole pasteurized milk of two milkings. After coagulation the curds are cut into small pieces and placed in wooden hoops to drain naturally, with the warm morning curds in the middle and the cool evening curds on the outside. The curds are salted and turned at regular intervals over a period of about two weeks, then ripened in a cool, humid environment for three to four months (a process that formerly took at least a year). The cheeses are usually sold wrapped in foil. Avoid any cheeses that are brownish or hard or that have a sour, bitter smell. Contrary to popular imagination, Gorgonzola should have a sharp, clean smell but not be overly pungent. Usually eaten as a dessert cheese with bread (and no butter), but there are some local culinary specialities, notably the Milanese *pere ripiene*, a delicious combination of pears stuffed with Gorgonzola. Also an ingredient of *pasta ai quattro formaggi*: pasta coated in a rich mixture of four cheeses, flavoured with sage and garlic. See *Dolcelatte*, *Stracchino*, *Torta Gaudenzio*

Gorgonzola Bianco
Rare, unveined white Gorgonzola. Also called Pannerone.

Grana ★   32%
The generic name Grana describes all those finely grained hard cheeses that originated in the Po valley and can be documented as far back as the 11th century. The most famous member of the group is undoubtedly Parmigiano Reggiano (Parmesan). All Grana cheese is made from partly skimmed milk and is matured in its distinctive drum shapes for at least a year. It is usually used as a grating cheese but when younger is also a delicious dessert cheese. Grana cheese should never be stored in the refrigerator; it keeps best covered with a cloth or greased paper in a cool cupboard or larder. For grating, buy a fair-sized chunk and grate it as and when you need it: this way it will release much more flavour and is ultimately more economical than the small

packets of ready-grated cheese. In Italian cooking there is really no substitute for Grana. Practically every *primo piatto* (first course) whether it be soup or *pasta* owes its success to a sprinkling of some sort of Grana on top. See *Emiliano, Grana Padano, Lodigiano, Parmigiano Reggiano*

Grana Bagozzo see *Bagozzo*

Grana Padano ★   ➤ 32%   24–40kg (53–88lb)

For centuries the cheese-producing centres of the Po valley wrangled over whose name should be associated with the excellent Grana they produced. Piacenza, long famed for its cheese 'il piacentino' and considered the most deserving contender, finally lost the battle when a compromise solution was reached in 1955. The names Grana Padano and Parmigiano Reggiano were given legal protection and the characteristics and area of production (*zona tipica*) of each cheese were precisely delineated. The qualifying provinces for Grana Padano were Alessandria, Asti, Cuneo, Novara, Turin, Vercelli, Bergamo, Brescia, Como, Cremona, Mantua (on the left bank of the Po), Milan, Pavia, Sondrio, Varese, Trento, Padua, Rovigo, Treviso, Venice, Verona, Vicenza, Bologna (on the right bank of the Reno), Ferrara, Forlì, Piacenza and Ravenna. Grana Padano is made all the year round and matures more rapidly but, apart from that, its characteristics are basically the same as those of Parmigiano Reggiano. It is a pressed cooked cheese made from partly skimmed milk of two milkings. The ripening period varies from one to two years and the cheeses are sold at varying stages of their maturity. The paste is a pale straw colour darkening with age. The rind is thick, oily and very hard and can be black or yellow-ochre in colour. See *Grana, Parmigiano Reggiano*

Italian cheeses have as many moods as Italian literature, and we can thus choose our luncheon reading to match them exactly.
      Edward & Lorna Bunyard THE EPICURE'S COMPANION

Groviera, Gruviera
The Italian version of Gruyère.

Incanestrato see *Canestrato*

Italico
The official designation invented in 1941 for a range of semi-soft delicately flavoured table cheeses similar to Bel Paese.

Lodigiano   ➤ 29%   30–50kg (66–110lb)
A Grana cheese produced around Lodi near Milan. The paste, typically hard and granular although more crumbly than Parmesan, is characterized by a slight greenish tinge. It is matured even longer than Parmesan, up to five years in some cases, and is extremely strong, even bitter to taste. It is also prohibitively expensive.

Logudoro   ➤ 50%   2kg (4lb)
Mild sweet factory-made dessert cheese from Lombardy. The paste is creamy white and there is no rind apart from wicker mould marks. Ripened for three to four weeks.

Majocchino
Ewes' milk cheese similar to Canestrato, made on a small scale in Sicily near Messina.

Manteca, Manteche
Cheeses similar to Burrini but larger, with a lump of butter encased in a coating of *pasta filata*, either Mozzarella, Provolone or Caciocavallo. The butter is usually whey butter made as a by-product of the two latter cheeses. Made in a variety of shapes (loaf, pear, ball, etc.) and sometimes smoked. The cheese jacket preserves the butter—a useful device in a hot climate before refrigeration was common. Originally from Basilicata.

**TORTA
san gaudenzio**

Ditta D. GALBANI & F. V.le MANZONI 10
NOVARA

Layers of Mascarpone
and Gorgonzola. Delicious

Mascarpone, Mascherpone ★   🧀 ⏃ 90% ● ◖
Delectable, virtually solidified cream, mildly acidulated by lactic fermentation and whipped up into a luscious velvety consistency. Originally produced in Lombardy only in the cool of autumn and winter but now available all year round. Sold in muslin bags and served fresh with candied or fresh fruit or flavoured with sugar, cinnamon, powdered chocolate or coffee and liqueurs. See *Torta Gaudenzio*

Montasio   🧀 ● 35% ⊖ 7–12kg (15–26½lb) ◗
Produced in northern Italy from partly skimmed milk, it is similar to Asiago, springy when young, hard and brittle after a year or two. Originally a monastery cheese (devised by monks at Moggio in the 13th century), it is now made in small cheese factories mostly in Udine and Veneto.

Montecenisio
Rare blue-veined cheese made from cows' or goats' milk on the Italian-French border.

Mozzarella   🧀 ⏃ 45% ● Ⓐ
The colonization of half the world by pizza chains has made Mozzarella the best-known Italian cheese after Parmesan and Gorgonzola. Melted on top of pizza it becomes quite palatable and is wonderfully stringy. In other respects, however, its flavour is one of the least interesting, especially if judged by the insipid factory product (often not Italian-made) available in most supermarkets. Choose Italian Mozzarella whenever possible and, for the best results, eat it the Italian way, dressed with olive oil, salt and freshly ground pepper and accompanied by tomatoes, olives, chillis, anchovies or even a sharp citrus fruit. Better still, if you can find it, is the original Mozzarella di Bufala (made from the milk of water buffaloes usually mixed with cows' milk) which is still made in parts of the south. This is softer, stickier and less rubbery than cows' milk Mozzarella and has a much stronger flavour and a more pronounced smell.

Mozzarella, which dates back to the 16th century, is a fresh *pasta filata* cheese, hand-moulded into creamy white balls and, in Italy, sold swimming in a bowl of whey. Elsewhere the cheese is wrapped in parchment or greaseproof paper or sealed into plastic bags with a little whey. Ideally it should be eaten as soon as possible after buying, but it will keep for a day or two if it is moistened with a little fresh milk and put in the refrigerator. Although Mozzarella is now made all over Italy (and in Denmark, England, and the United States among other places) the best is reputedly that from Capua, Cardito, Aversa and the Sele valley. A lightly smoked version called Mozzarella Affumicata is also available.

Apart from pizza, Mozzarella is used in the making of many dishes including *lasagne*, *supplì* (rice balls with cheese in the middle) and the ubiquitous *mozzarella in carrozza* (a sandwich of bread and cheese dipped in beaten egg and milk and fried). See *Fior di Latte*, *Scamorza*

Nostrale
Simple locally made rustic cheese. The name denotes not so much a particular cheese type as the fact that it is 'home-made' or made in the locality.

Ovoli
Egg-shaped Mozzarella cheeses.

Pagliarini
Small, medium-ripened, softish cheeses from Piedmont, usually somewhat sour-tasting. Sold on little straw mats (*paglia*, straw), they are often eaten dressed with oil and seasoned.

Panedda see *Casigliolo*
Pannarone, Pannerone see *Gorgonzola Bianco*
Pannerino see *Stracchino*
Parmesan see *Parmigiano Reggiano*

Parmigiano Reggiano ★ 🐄 🥛 32% 🧀 30kg (66lb) ● ❺
The heavyweight champion of the cheese world, better known as Parmesan, yet how many people have tasted this wonderful cheese only as a commercialized, prepacked powder. The whole cheese is a truly magnificent sight: an enormous shiny brown drum with its name stamped vertically all over the sides. When split open (along the natural grain of the cheese using a special leaf-shaped knife), it reveals a beautiful straw-yellow grainy paste, brittle and crumbly with a superb fruity flavour that should never be bitter. It has been lauded by name for at least 700 years, but the Grana family of cheeses to which it belongs has a much more ancient provenance. Grana was being made in Italy even before the advent of the Romans and has long been valued for both medicinal and gastronomic purposes. (Molière is said to have lived largely on Parmesan during his declining years.)

The making of Parmigiano Reggiano is strictly controlled. It has to be made between 1 April and 11 November with milk from the *zona tipica* (the provinces of Parma, Reggio Emilia, Modena, Mantua on the right bank of the Po and Bologna on the left bank of the Reno). Unpasteurized evening and morning milk are partly skimmed and then mixed together in huge copper cauldrons. The starter is added and the milk brought gradually up to a temperature of 33°C (91°F) when the rennet is added to coagulate the milk over a period of about 15 minutes. The curds are then broken up with a sharp rod (*spino*) into tiny grains, which are then cooked in the whey at 55°C (131°F), left to settle on the bottom of the vat, scooped out in a cheese cloth and pressed in a special mould (*fascera*). The cheeses are left in these moulds for several days and then salted in brine for about three weeks before being stored for at least one and no more than four years. The cheeses are sold at four stages of their maturation: *giovane* (young, after a year), *vecchio* (old, after two years), *stravecchio* (mature, after three years) and *stravecchione* (extra mature, after four years). Parmigiano is at the peak of perfection when it is *con gocciola*, which means that when the cheese is split open you can just see tiny tears of moisture glistening on the surface. It is a superb dessert cheese when young and as it gets older it is grated and sprinkled on *pasta asciutta*, *risotto* and innumerable other dishes. See *Grana*

. . . and on a mountain, all of grated Parmesan cheese, dwell folk that do nought else but make macaroni and raviuoli, and boil them, in capon's broth . . .
Giovanni Boccaccio THE DECAMERON

Passito

A Stracchino made from summer milk. The paste is less moist and more compact with a rather acid taste compared to the traditional winter-made stracchino.

Pecorino ★

Generic name for ewes' milk cheeses (from *pecora*, sheep)—one of the most important Italian cheese families and particularly associated with central and southern Italy. A typical Pecorino is a hand-pressed, cooked, drum- or wheel-shaped cheese, made from whole or skimmed unpasteurized milk coagulated with sheep's rennet, and decidedly piquant in flavour. The farther south one goes, the more *piccante* the cheeses become. Any ewes' milk cheese can be called a Pecorino and there are many local variations and a bewildering prolixity of names and designations for what are basically similar cheeses. Over the centuries some have become more widely known and more important commercially than others, notably Pecorino Romano and Pecorino Siciliano.

Pecorino Pepato

A Pecorino (usually Siciliano) flavoured with whole black peppercorns, sometimes simply called Pepato.

Pecorino Romano ★   36% ⬡6–22kg (13–48lb)

The most famous of the Pecorino cheeses and the legendary cheese made by Romulus, Pecorino Romano had its characteristics and *zona tipica* precisely laid down by the Stresa Convention of 1951. Made between November and June, the traditional area of production is Lazio, but this has now been extended to include Sardinia.

Pecorino Romano has always been a popular cheese both in Italy and overseas. Columella talks of it being exported in the 1st century AD and a considerable amount of the cheese produced today finds it way abroad, especially to the United States. It has a greyish-white close-textured paste and a dark brown or black very hard rind rubbed with oil and wood ash or wax or a yellow clay-based compound. It is ripened for a minimum of eight months, when the flavour is sharp and dry and goes particularly well with coarse country bread. Grated, it is an essential part of many regional dishes. It gives off a somewhat acrid smell when sprinkled on hot food, but this should be tolerated in the interests of authenticity; the flavour is not adversely affected. See *Pecorino*, *Pecorino Sardo*

Pecorino Sardo

The traditional Sardinian Pecorino, made with whole or skimmed ewes' milk. Its characteristics are basically the same as Pecorino Romano since the processing is identical. The slight variations in flavour are a result of inevitable local differences in the milk. True connoisseurs can tell the two cheeses apart, unlike most of the rest of us. If anything, they say, Sardo is drier and slightly more *piccante* than Romano.

Pecorino Senese

A type of Pecorino Toscano made near Siena. The rind is rubbed with tomato paste or with olive oil and wood ash.

Pecorino Siciliano see *Canestrato*
Pecorino Toscano see *Toscanello*
Pepato see *Pecorino Pepato*
Pera di Vacca see *Casigliolo*

Piacentino

Once a Grana cheese made in Piacenza. Now refers to a small long-ripened Sicilian Pecorino used for grating.

Pressato ☼ ➧ 30% ⊖ 9–14kg (20–31lb) ⬤

Firm, yellow, cooked cheese with many uneven holes spread throughout the paste, made from partly skimmed milk. It was first developed in Vicenza as a variant of Asiago. Pressato is a more even-tempered cheese than Asiago and, at least locally, is now more popular. Unlike Asiago, it is salted partly before and partly after being pressed, it ripens in a much shorter time— about 40 days maximum—and is eaten only as a dessert cheese. The flavour is pleasantly sweet and fragrant.

Provatura

Small, fresh, spun-curd cheese like Mozzarella, once made from buffalo milk, now from cows' milk. *Crostini di provatura* are circles of bread covered with cheese and anchovies and baked.

Provola, Provole

Can be either unripened Provolone moulded into small balls or longer ripened Mozzarella. The cheese is soft, sweet and mild with a hard wax coating. Burrini are sometimes sold under this name and Provola is sometimes sold under a brand name (e.g. Ciccillo). To add to the confusion, a variety of other diminutives may be used (such as Provolette or Provolini), but they are all basically the same (literally, tiny Provoloni). Also available smoked (*affumicata*).

Provolone ★ ☼ ➧ 44% 200g–30kg (7oz–66lb) ⬤ ⬤

An uncooked, smooth, close-textured *pasta filata* cheese made from whole cows' milk coagulated with calf's rennet (Provolone Dolce) or kid's rennet (Provolone Piccante). Originated in southern Italy, but production has now spread to the Po valley and with it the increasingly pervasive trend (much deprecated by connoisseurs) towards the mild (*dolce*) rather than the piquant (*piccante*) varieties. The former, aged for two to three months, is softer, mild and smooth with a thin waxed rind. The latter, aged from six months to two years, is darker in colour with small eyes, a tough hard rind and a stronger spicier flavour. Hand-moulded into multifarious shapes, and sold under a diversity of names, such as Ercolini, Silanetti, Sorrentini (the smaller ones) and Pancette, Pancettoni, Salami, Giganti, Gigantoli (their big brothers). The larger cheeses are sometimes smoked and are usually bound with raffia or string and hung up in pairs on poles while waiting to be sold. The best come from Campania and Puglia.

Quartirolo

🎋 🐄 48% ●

From Lombardy, an uncooked pressed cheese with a pale paste and thin washed rind. Nowadays it is made all year round but at one time only in autumn from the fourth growth of grass, *erba quartirolo*, hence the name.

Ragusano

From Ragusa, Sicily, whose flowery meadows produce fine-quality milk with a high fat content and give this *pasta filata* cows' milk cheese its particular flavour and aroma. It can either be steeped in brine and aged for up to six months as a table cheese, or ripened longer, when the rind is rubbed with olive oil, to produce a grating cheese with a strong, spicy flavour.

The first dish is a cabbage, boiled with a great quantity of rice in a tureen full of water, and flavoured with cheese. It is so hot and we are so cold that it appears almost jolly.
Charles Dickens PICTURES FROM ITALY

Raveggiolo

A creamy white ewes' milk cheese with a slightly elastic texture. Eaten within a few weeks of making.

Ricotta ★

Traditionally a whey cheese, but nowadays whole or skimmed milk is sometimes added, giving a much richer product. It is white and mild with a fine, granular consistency and is usually shaped like an upturned basin with basketwork marks on the outside. Ricotta Romana, Toscana, Sarda and Siciliana are made from ewes' milk whey (left over from making Pecorino). Ricotta Piemontese is made from cows' milk whey and is smoother and slightly more bland. There are three types: the most familiar *tipo dolce* is bland, very soft, unripened and unsalted; *tipo moliterno* is salted and dried; *tipo forte* is matured to a dry hard consistency and used mostly for grating. Fresh Ricotta is used a great deal in Italian cooking: it can be mixed with spinach and made into *gnocchi* or used as a filling for *ravioli* and *cannelloni*; it makes a delicious base for cheesecake and is also often eaten fresh, sprinkled with powdered coffee or chocolate, or with sugar and fresh fruit. Ricotta laced with brandy or rum is called in Tuscany *Ricotta ubriaca* (drunken Ricotta). Ricotta can also be called Brocotte. See *Canestrato*

Rob(b)iola

Another of those confusing designations that can mean a number of different things. The name has two possible derivations: from the Lombardy village of Robbio in Lomellina and from the Latin *rubium*, red, an indication of the reddish-brown rind typical of most Robiola cheeses. It usually means a soft, unpressed cows' milk cheese that ripens over a period of one to four weeks, when it acquires the characteristic red mould coating. This cheese resembles Taleggio and becomes gradually more piquant with age. Another rarer type is more akin to Camembert, ripened for no more than a few weeks and becoming softer and creamier with age. The name is also applied to some Caciotta-type cheeses, especially those from Piedmont and Liguria.

Robiolette, Robiolini
Small cheeses from Lombardy, usually shaped into rolls or bars, slightly acid to taste and eaten with oil and seasoning.

Romano
Italians always distinguish between Pecorino Romano (made with ewes' milk), Caprino Romano (made with goats' milk) and Vacchino Romano (made with cows' milk). Outside Italy, Romano refers to cows' milk cheese. Like Pecorino Romano it is hard and sharp and eaten both young and matured.

The label is not too fanciful—Taleggio is an old type once made in alpine valleys in winter

A cheese now made by the Galbani factory in Melzo

San Gaudenzio see *Torta Gaudenzio*

Scamorza
From Abruzzi, a type of cows' milk Mozzarella. The word means 'dunce' in southern dialect.

Scanno
Table Pecorino from Abruzzi. Traditionally eaten with fresh fruit. Black on the outside and buttery yellow inside. The flavour has a mildly burnt tinge.

Stracchino   48%   50g–4kg (1½oz–9lb)
Stracchino is a generic term for a type of Lombardy cheese that was at one time made in the autumn and winter from the milk of cows that had come down from their summer alpine pastures to be wintered on the plains. The milk of these 'tired' cows (*stracche* in the Lombardy dialect) imparted a distinctive flavour to the cheese (as a result of the change of grazing). They were also quick-ripening cheeses that in the days before refrigeration could be made only in the winter. Nowadays these cheeses are made all year round and many different types come under the same etymological umbrella. Gorgonzola is a Stracchino. So are Taleggio and some Robiola cheeses. Frequently they are sold under brand names such as Certosa, Certosino, Stracchinella, Invernizzina, Pannerino, etc. A typical representative

of this group of cheeses, Stracchino-Crescenza is square-shaped, rindless, white and lusciously creamy with a rather gentle luxurious flavour. It is ripened for a maximum of ten days and should be eaten as soon as possible after that. The best Crescenza reputedly comes from around Milan and Pavia.

Taleggio ★   ⌬ 🐄 48% ⬭ 2kg (4lb) 🐄

Named after a small town near Bergamo, this is an unpressed uncooked cheese of the Stracchino type. The paste is white and supple with a thin pinkish-grey rind that should never be cracked or broken. The cheese ripens in about 40 days, when the flavour is mild and fruity. Under perfect conditions some cheeses can be ripened for twice as long: the flavour deepens, the cheese becomes plumper, more aromatic and the paste a deeper yellow. These and Taleggio made with unpasteurized milk are especially prized.

Toma, Tuma

Fresh, white, bland cheese, usually eaten after a meal, dressed with olive oil, pepper and salt. From Piedmont.

Torta (San) Gaudenzio ★

One of several trade names for Gorgonzola con Mascarpone: alternate layers of these two cheeses pressed together like a gâteau. The mixture of Gorgonzola and Mascarpone is a traditional one, originating in the Trieste area, where it may also be flavoured with anchovy and caraway seeds. Also called Torta Gorgonzola.

Toscanello

Tuscan cheese made either from ewes' milk or a mixture of ewes' and cows' milk. Small firm cheeses with a pale golden paste and smooth rind. Eaten as a table cheese after a few months or aged for grating. Also called Caciotta Toscana when made with mixed milk, and Pecorino Toscano when made entirely with ewes' milk.

Trecce, Treccia

Plaited type of Mozzarella.

Tuma see *Toma*
Vacchino Romano see *Romano*

Vezzena

Rare Grana-type cheese related to Asiago though very much sharper and without the holes. The grainy paste ranges from white (winter-made cheeses) to yellow (summer-made). Eaten after six months as a table cheese and after a year or more for grating. Also called Veneto, Venezza.

Key words	
Affumicato smoked	**Molle** soft
Bufala buffalo	**Mucca** milk cow
Cacio old word for cheese	**Pecora** ewe
Capra goat	**Piccante** piquant
Dolce mild	**Vacca** cow
Duro hard	**Vecchio** old
Formaggio cheese	**Zona tipica** area of production
Fresco fresh	**Stravecchio** mature
Giovane young	**Stravecchione** extra mature

Latin America

Cheesemaking was unknown to the indigenous Amerindians before the Europeans arrived in Latin America some 500 years ago. European breeds of cattle and sheep, brought over by the colonizers, did not generally adapt well to new conditions, and even where they did (in Argentina, for example) dairying took second place to the production of meat. Most of Latin America falls within the tropical zone, not renowned for its particularly inspiring cheese types. Simple fresh cheeses are commonplace and some unsophisticated versions of popular European types are made on a commercial basis. Untemperamental long-keeping cheeses like Dutch Edam and Gouda have proved widely adaptable throughout Latin America, and Argentina makes very acceptable imitations of several Italian types including Parmesan, Mozzarella and Romano.

Añejo (Mexico)
Dry salty goat cheese, ripened for eight months. Sometimes covered with chilli powder and called Queso Enchilado.

Asadero (Mexico)
Literally 'good for roasting', a *pasta filata* cheese made from whole cows' milk. From the south. Also called Oaxaca.

Bernina (Colombia)
Piquant soft cows' milk cheese ripened for about a week.

Campesino (Paraguay)
Fresh, lightly pressed, salty cows' milk cheese.

Catupiri (Brazil)
Rennet-curd cows' milk cheese eaten with quince marmalade.

Chanco (Chile) 🐄 50% ⬭ 6–10kg (13–22lb)
Named after a small coastal town south of Santiago. Smooth, mild buttery cheese with a golden-brown rind made mostly from pasteurized milk. Also called Mantecoso.

Chihuahua (Mexico)
Soft, sourish cows' milk cheese much used in cooking.

Cincho (Venezuela)
Fresh acid-curd ewes' milk cheese like Spanish Villalón.

Coyolito (El Salvador) 🐄 ⬭ 20–22kg (44–48lb)
Coarse, piquant, pressed cheese washed with brine and coconut milk during a three-week ripening period.

Crema (Argentina) 🐑 55% ⬭ 3·8kg (8lb)
Fresh soft cream cheese ripened for about a week.

Cuajada (Venezuela)
Cows' milk curd cheese wrapped in maize or banana leaves.

Gaucho (Argentina)
Semi-hard cows' milk cheese made from skimmed milk.

Hoja (Puerto Rico)
Brined cows' milk cheese thinly rolled and folded in layers.

Llanero (Venezuela)
Strong, crumbly, grating cheese from the *llanos*, huge plains stretching south of Caracas into Colombia.

Maduro (Costa Rica)
Semi-hard low-fat cheese made from pasteurized cows' milk.

Mano (Venezuela)
Pasta filata cows' milk cheese wrapped in banana leaves.

Mantecoso (Peru, Chile)
In Peru a popular farm-made soft cheese. In Chile a semi-hard cheese similar to European monastery types. See *Chanco*

Minas (Brazil) ☒ ☽ 42% ⊖ 500g–3kg (18oz–7lb) ● ℂ
Bland, slightly sour acid-curd cheese made in small factories in Minas Gerais from whole pasteurized milk. Sold either fresh (*frescal*) or pressed and partly ripened (*prensado*). Used in cooking and eaten for breakfast and as a dessert with candied fruit or preserves.

Oaxaca see *Asadero*

Patagras (Cuba) ☒ ☾ 40% ⊖ 5kg (11lb) ℂ
Springy, mild, firm cheese with a red waxed rind similar to Gouda. Made from whole or partly skimmed pasteurized milk.

Pera (Colombia)
Small, fairly hard spun-curd cheese made from partly skimmed cows' milk and stuffed with candied fruit.

Petacones (El Salvador)
Hard-pressed cows' milk cheeses ripened for about two weeks.

Prato (Brazil)
The name, meaning 'plate', derives from the original shape of the cheese. One of the most popular Brazilian types. Made from cows' milk, it is a mild, soft, pressed cheese with a deep golden waxed rind. Ripened for six to seven weeks.

Quartirolo (Argentina, Brazil)
Soft fresh cheese made from cows' milk, like Mozzarella.

Quesillos (Chile, Paraguay)
Small, soft, fresh cows' milk cheeses wrapped in banana or maize leaves.

Queso Blanco
Generic term for fresh white cheese produced throughout Latin America from whole or skimmed milk or whey.

Queso Enchilado see *Añejo*

Reino (Brazil)
Similar to Portuguese Serra cheese but softer and milder.

Requeijão (Brazil)
Bland, soft, skimmed-milk, acid-curd cows' milk cheese.

Suero (Costa Rica)
Low-fat cheese made from buttermilk.

Middle East

Good pasture is difficult to find in most Middle Eastern countries so the most important milk-producers are goats and ewes—well-adapted to foraging for food in unpromising terrain. Cheeses—mostly white brined types—are simple but very popular, especially for breakfast.

'Akkawī (Lebanon)
Fresh, soft, white cows' milk cheese.

Baida (Egypt)
A white pressed cheese made from skimmed cows' or buffalo milk. Eaten fresh or cured in its own whey.

Baladī (Lebanon)
White crumbly cheese made from ewes' or cows' milk. Eaten fresh, salted or unsalted.

Beyaz Peynir (Turkey)
Literally 'white cheese', made of ewes' milk, sometimes mixed with goats' milk. Eaten in great quantities especially for breakfast, either fresh or ripened in brine for up to seven months. Similar to Greek Feta.

Biza (Iraq)
Fresh acid-curd cheese made from hand-skimmed ewes' milk. Flavoured with garlic, onion or carob. Also called Fajy.

Danni (Egypt)
Ewes' milk cheese from northern Egypt. Eaten after three days or ripened in its whey for four to five months.

Dil Peyniri (Turkey)
Hard, round, spun-curd cheese made from any type of milk.

Dumyātī (Egypt)
Egypt's most popular cheese is made from whole cows' or buffalo milk. Unusually, the milk is salted before, rather than after, renneting. Sold either fresh—soft, white and mild in flavour—or ripened for four to eight months in salted whey or brine when it becomes darker in colour and very much more tangy and salty. Named after a port on the Nile delta. Packed in tins for export.

Edirne (Turkey)
Soft fresh ewes' milk cheese made in the north-west.

Fajy see *Biza*

Gibne, Jibne
Simple cheese found all over the Middle East, traditionally made by nomads. Ewes', goats' or camels' milk is coagulated with animal or vegetable rennet. Eaten fresh.

Gravyer (Turkey)
Turkish imitation of Gruyère.

Jubna (Saudi Arabia)
Fresh, white, round, heavily salted cheese made from ewes' or goats' milk. Eaten after pressing or preserved in brine.

Kareish (Egypt)
Acid-curd very salty cheese made from skimmed cows' or buffalo milk. Eaten fresh or ripened in brine.

Kaşar, Kaşer (Turkey)
Pressed semi-hard cheese usually made from ewes' milk but sometimes from cows' milk or a mixture of the two.

Kashkawān (Lebanon, Syria)
Pressed spun-curd cheese made from goats' milk, similar to Italian Caciocavallo. Ripened for six to seven weeks.

Labna (Lebanon)
Fresh, soft, acid-curd cheese made from any kind of milk.

Labniya (Syria)
Sour-milk curds thickened with rice or barley meal, flavoured with herbs and steeped in oil. It can be called cheese—but only just. Most Syrian cheeses are made at home for domestic use.

Lor (Turkey)
Fresh cheese made from ewes' milk whey mixed with whole milk.

Meira (Iraq)
Semi-hard cheese with good keeping qualities made from ewes' milk, pressed between heavy stones and ripened in sheepskins for up to a year.

Mihalıççık (Turkey)
Semi-hard ewes' milk cheese salted in a brine bath for two weeks and ripened for about three months.

Mīsh (Egypt)
Fresh goats' milk 'started' with a piece of mature Mīsh and salted, spiced and aged for about a year in earthenware pots. Extremely salty, even for the Middle East.

Roos (Iraq)
Strong, salty cheese made from ewes' or goats' milk near Ain Kawa and Haj Omran. Moulded and pressed by hand into balls and ripened for about six months.

Salamura (Turkey)
Strong white goats' milk cheese ripened in brine.

Tel Peyniri (Turkey)
Same as Dil Peyniri but usually made from skimmed ewes' milk.

Tulum Peyniri (Turkey)
Semi-hard pressed cheese made of partly skimmed ewes' or goats' milk mixed with olive oil or yoghurt and ripened for about four months in a sheepskin or goatskin bag (a *tulum*). Very dry, strong and pungent.

Van Peyniri (Turkey)
Goats' milk cheese from Lake Van. Fresh, white and crumbly when young, becoming brown and powdery with age. Stored in goatskin bags. May also be herb-flavoured. Eaten for breakfast.

MOROCCO see *Africa*.

The Netherlands

Dutch cheeses, although few in number, have achieved a spectacular commercial success, so much so that the Netherlands and cheese are automatically associated in many people's minds. The Netherlands are, in fact, by far the largest exporters of cheese in the world, a position they have held for centuries. At an early date Dutch cheesemakers developed cheeses with exceptional keeping qualities, ones that were easily transportable and reliable rather than exotic—cheeses typified by Gouda and Edam. Both are now among the most copied cheese types in the world, along with English Cheddar, French Camembert and Swiss 'Swiss'. The tangy, strongly spiced cheeses have proved less popular abroad, although much liked by the Dutch themselves.

Cheesemaking in the Netherlands is heavily industrialized. Fewer than 100 fully automated factories turn out nearly 500 million kg (approximately 1,100 million lb) of cheese each year with a bare minimum of staff. Computerized cheesemaking has led to a decline in the number of farmhouse producers, most of whom make Goudas and Leidens, to about a fifth of the immediate postwar figure. There are very few local cheeses: some ewes' milk cheeses on the island of Texel and in the province of Friesland and some goats' milk cheeses in Ankeveen, Noord-Holland and Aarle-Rixtel, Brabant.

The Dutch are great consumers as well as exporters of cheese. They eat it after meals and for breakfast, often fried with potatoes, but apart from this, it is used surprisingly rarely in Dutch cuisine.

Amsterdammer see *Gouda*

Cessibon
Trade name for a mild, soft, creamy cows' milk cheese similar to Mon Chou.

Commissiekaas see *Edam*

Dietkaas
Similar to Gouda and produced especially for those on low-salt diets. Fat content ranges between 20 and 48 per cent and it is distinguished by a 'D' on the control stamp.

Edam (Edammer) ★
🐄 🌢 40% ○ 880g–6·5kg (31oz–14lb) 🐄

Its shiny bright red coating of paraffin wax makes Edam the most immediately recognizable cheese in the world (although in the Netherlands itself the cheeses are sold with the natural golden rind uncovered). Its equally distinctive perfect spherical shape occurs because the cheese firms quickly before the interior has time to settle. Edam is smooth and supple with a slightly acidulous aftertaste, sold young, at about three or four months old, or after a year or so, when it becomes stronger, drier and saltier. It is entirely factory-made and may sometimes be flavoured with cumin seeds.

Edam originated in the town of Edam at least 600 years ago and has always been highly successful commercially. By the late 17th century about 454,000 kg (1,000,000 lb) of cheese was being exported every year, much of it to the Dutch colonies. Some of these countries have used it to produce wonderfully exotic dishes, such as *keshy yena* from the Dutch Antilles—a cheese stuffed with fish or meat and vegetables and baked whole. Edam's excellent keeping properties make it particularly suitable for warmer climates, and not only, it seems, for eating. One story insists that the Uruguayans once defeated the Argentinians in a naval battle by substituting aged Edams for cannonballs. Such old hard cheeses are now rarely found, but Edam is sold in several different versions to suit contemporary tastes. The normal size weighs around 1.7kg (3½lb). There is also a smaller Baby Edam, a stronger double-sized Commissiekaas (sold as Mimolette in France and coloured deep orange with annatto), and Middelbaar, a heavyweight at 6·5kg (14lb).

Friese Nagelkaas   🌱 ➋ 20–40% 😐 7–9kg (15–20lb) 🐄

Surprisingly, the homeland of the ubiquitous black and white Friesian cattle has not produced many original cheese types. Nagelkaas (literally 'nail cheese') is a rather coarse, hardpressed, long-ripening cheese made from whole milk sometimes mixed with buttermilk and studded with cloves and cumin seeds. Sometimes sold as Friesian Clove. The paste is greywhite, dry and extremely spicy and piquant after a minimum of six months' ageing. The rind is tough and hard, especially in well-matured cheeses. Friese Kanterkaas is the same cheese without spices.

The quality control stamp for factory-made Gouda.

The quality control stamp for farmhouse Gouda

Gouda (Goudsche) ★

🌱 ➋ 48% 😐 2·5–20kg (5½–44lb) 🐄 🅰

The most important Dutch cheese, accounting for over two-thirds of the total production, which originated in Gouda in the 13th century. Made from full milk, it is a pressed uncooked cheese with a firm straw-coloured paste scattered with small irregular holes or a few large ones depending on the type of starter culture that has been used. The young cheeses, aged for one to four months, are very mild and buttery, but mature Goudas, sometimes ripened for as long as a year, are darker in colour and much tangier, with a fuller, richer flavour and a more pronounced spicy aroma. These mature Goudas can also be farmhouse cheeses made from unpasteurized milk, in which case they will have the word *Boeren* (*boer*, farmer) stamped on the rind. There are still about 1,000 farms in Zuid-Holland and Utrecht making Gouda by traditional methods, even though most is now factory-made. In earlier days farmers brought their cheeses every Thursday morning to the cheese market at Gouda outside the 17th-century cheese weigh-house (*Kaaswag*) and, after a ritual bargaining over price, the deals were customarily sealed with a slapping of hands (*handje-klap*). Nowadays a version of this ceremony is presented for tourists.

Gouda is produced in various sizes. The smallest, Baby Gouda or Lunchkaas, is usually eaten young, after four weeks' ripening, and is factory- and farmhouse-made. Amsterdammer, ripened for four to eight weeks, is a small, softer, creamier Gouda with a higher moisture content than usual and a distinctive shiny orange rind. There is also a version flavoured with cumin seeds. Gouda is an excellent cooking cheese at all stages of its maturity: it is used as a melting cheese when young, especially in the *kaasdoop*, the Dutch version of fondue, and as a grating cheese when older. Traditionally eaten with brown bread and boiled potatoes.

Kanterkaas see *Friese Nagelkaas*

Kernhem (Kernhemse) ★   🐄 🧈 60% 😀 1·6kg (3½lb) 🍴

Washed-rind cheese reminiscent of traditional monastery cheeses but recently invented by the Netherlands Institute of Dairy Research. Made from slightly pasteurized milk with an augmented fat content. It is lightly pressed and ripened for about four weeks in cool humid conditions, during which time it is regularly turned and the rind washed with water. The paste is creamy and golden in colour, with a full, rich flavour. Kernhem is classed by the Dutch as a *meshanger* cheese—one that clings to the knife when cut.

The Dutch cheesemaking industry still retains a pleasing regard for its traditional customs. There are several cheese markets well worth visiting, at Gouda, Bodegraven, Woerden, Purmerend and, in particular, that at Alkmaar, held on Friday mornings from May to September. Members of the Cheese Carriers' Guild dress in their 16th-century costumes: white suits and red, blue, green or yellow hats depending on the warehouse they represent. Goudas and Edams, like a heap of huge golden grapefruit, are stacked on painted wooden sleds, which are then carried by hand to the market-place.

Kwark

Soft, white, lightly drained fresh curd cheese. Used, in particular, in desserts combined with fruit. The most popular Kwark (Magere Kwark) is made from skimmed milk and the fat content is practically nil.

Leerdammer see *Maasdam*

Leiden, Leyden ★   🐄 🥛 20–40% 😀 4–12kg (9–26½lb) 🍴
(Leidse)

Pressed, uncooked, crumbly, rather salty cheese made from partly skimmed milk and buttermilk and flavoured with cumin seeds. Modern cheesemaking hygiene forbids the traditional practice of treading the cumin into the curds: feet have been replaced by machines. Leiden is ripened for at least three months. Factory-made cheeses have natural yellow rinds but farmhouse Leidens have their rinds rubbed with annatto (at one time a mixture of vegetable dye and beestings was used), making them a deep, glowing orange-red. Farmhouse Leiden (stamped with the words *Boeren Leidse* and a pair of crossed keys, the arms of the city of Leiden) has a legal minimum fat content of 30 per cent (although usually higher in practice) and is drier and sharper than the factory version, which has a fat content of 40 or, occasionally, 20 per cent.

Lunchkaas see *Gouda*

Maasdam 🌀 ● 45% ⬭ 12–13kg (26–28lb) 🍴
A factory-made, recently developed cheese similar to Swiss Emmental. It has a firm, plump, golden body with many large holes caused by the action of propionic acid bacteria added to the curds. Ripened for at least four weeks. The flavour is sweetish and mildly nutty. Commonly sold under trade names such as Westberg and Leerdammer.

Middelbaar see *Edam*

Mimolette see *Edam*

Mon Chou 🌀 🌙 73% ▱ 100g (3½oz) 🍴
Rich, creamy, factory-made cheese with a mild, faintly acid flavour. Sold wrapped in foil; of recent origin.

Pompadour 🌀 ● 48–50% ⬭ 4kg (9lb) 🍴
Trade name for a new, smooth, creamy cheese made in several versions: Naturel (mild with a white rind), Rouge (mild, coloured red with annatto, white rind), Pikant (sharp, ripened for 12 weeks, brown rind), Alt (very strong, ripened for 24 weeks, black rind). Also flavoured with caraway seeds (yellow rind) or herbs (green rind).

Subenhara 🌀 🌙 20–48% ⬭ 1kg (2lb) 🍴
Rich, soft, new factory-made cheese flavoured with garlic and herbs.

Texel
Rare, fresh ewes' milk cheese from the island of Texel. Rumour has it that the particular flavour of this cheese is, or at least was, a result of steeping sheep's droppings in the milk before coagulation.

Westberg see *Maasdam*

Witte Meikaas 🌀 🌙 48% ⬭ 2·5–5kg (5½–11lb) 🍴
Fresh white curd cheese with a high moisture content, made from whole milk and rather acid in flavour. The name means 'White May'. Made only by a few farms all year round, but especially in spring.

Key words

Belegen 4–6 months old	**Koe** cow
Boerenkaas farmhouse cheese	**Oude** over 9 months old
Extra belegen 6–9 months old	**Ryp** mature
Geit goat	**Schaap** ewe
Jong 4–8 weeks old	**Vers** fresh
Jong belegen 2–4 months old	**Volvet** full fat
Kaas cheese	**Zacht** soft

NEW ZEALAND see *Australasia*.

North America

UNITED STATES

North America has not, on the whole, been kind to cheese, although more cheese and more types of cheese are made there than anywhere else. Some are fine natural cheeses—genuine original American types and good foreign imitations—made and sold with the same care and discernment that typify the best European cheeses. These are unfortunately too often swamped by the mass of anaesthetized, homogenized, artificially coloured and flavoured, pre-packed, ready-sliced, ready-shredded, ready-grated—it sometimes seems ready-digested—cheese food and cheese products. Processed cheese—once described by Clifton Fadiman as 'the corpse of milk'—is prevalent all over the world, yet somehow even natural cheeses manage to taste processed in America. It often seems that the natural flavour of the cheese has been removed, only to be replaced by something inferior and often totally inappropriate. All American dairy products, even imported ones, are pasteurized, which may be part of the explanation. Additives and preservatives are rampant, but at least their must be stated on the packaging. It is not unusual to see a packet of 'Imitation Cheddar Cheese' bearing the ominous rubric 'contains Cheddar Cheese' followed by a list of 16 other ingredients. Yet there are signs that in America, as elsewhere, a revolt against over-packaged, over-processed food is growing. This can only be good news for cheeselovers as it means that more and better cheeses will become more widely available.

American 🏵 ⟩ 50% 🧀 🅒

A term loosely used to mean American-made Cheddar. American cheese is virtually synonymous with Cheddar. It represents over 70 per cent of America's gigantic production, was the first cheese brought to America (by the Pilgrim Fathers), the first to be made there and the first to be industrialized. Early farm-made cheeses were much praised by travellers, but factory production has now taken over entirely. American Cheddars, graded AA and A by the Department of Agriculture, come in all shapes and sizes and range from bland to medium strong. They are often heavily dyed with annatto and waxed black, red or orange. The various names under which the cheese is sold such as Barrel, Mammoth, Daisy, Picnic, Twin, Longhorn, Young American, refer usually to the size of the whole cheese, but there are also regional variants with different flavours, aromas and textures. See *Camosun, Colby, Coon, Cornhusker, Pineapple, Tillamook, Vermont*

American Blue 🏵 🐄 50% 🗆 2kg (4lb) 🅒

Based on Roquefort, but made from pasteurized cows' milk, to which *Penicillium roquefortii* has been added. Ripened for three to four months. Among the better brands are Maytag, Nauvoo and Oregon Blue.

Bakers

Simple, unripened, fresh, low-fat cheese made from skimmed cows' milk and much used in the bakery trade to make cheesecakes and pastries. Sloppier, smoother and rather more sour-tasting than Cottage Cheese, it is eaten fresh or may be deep-frozen and stored for several months. Occasionally made from skimmed milk powder. Best used for cooking.

Braided Cheese

Of Armenian origin, strips of fresh *pasta filata* cheese plaited or twisted together. Very white, rubbery and quite tasteless unless flavoured with caraway or nigella seeds (*Nigella damascena*, better known as Love-in-a-mist). Not usually eaten raw but often melted and used in cooking. Also called String Cheese.

Brick ★   ☼ ◑ 50% ▭ 2·5kg (5½lb) C

Truly original, a lightly pungent sweetish cheese with numerous holes in a very pale supple paste. Many think of it as a cross between Limburger and Cheddar, but it is really much more like Tilsit than anything else. It was invented in the 1870s by a Swiss cheesemaker in Wisconsin, where most of it is still made. The name derives from its shape or, some say, from the traditional practice of pressing it with bricks. The rind is smeared with a culture of *Bacterium linens* and regularly wiped with a cloth dipped in brine during the three-month ripening. The resulting aroma is distinctly spicy but not overpowering compared to other washed-rind cheeses. The reddish natural rind is sometimes removed and the cheeses waxed before they are sold. Sometimes described, obscurely, as 'the married man's Limburger'.

Camosun

Softish, crumbly, mild type of Cheddar invented in Washington State in 1932. Ripened for one to three months.

Chantelle

Full-fat, mild sliceable cows' milk cheese with a springy yellow paste similar to Italian Bel Paese. Coated in red wax.

Colby   ☼ ◑ 50% C

From Colby, Wisconsin, a Cheddar variant first made in 1882 by Ambrose and J.H. Steinwand. The curd is not 'cheddared', which makes the paste more open and granular than an ordinary Cheddar. It is dyed deep orange yellow and waxed or vacuum packed in variously sized blocks or rounds. The flavour is mild and rather sweet. A popular everyday cheese.

Coldpack

Somewhere between a natural and a processed cheese. A spread made by blending two or more cheeses with various other ingredients including water, vinegar, citric acid, colouring, spices, artificial smoky flavouring and herbs. The mixture is not heated as in the case of processed cheese, hence the name. Moulded in various shapes or packed in cartons, tubs, foil or pots and sometimes called Potted Cheese.

Coon

One of the strongest American Cheddars with a fully matured tangy flavour although in fact it is only ripened for two to three months. It has a dry, crumbly very pale paste and a dark brown rind. A very rare cheese from New York State.

Cornhusker

A rare, softer, milder springy Cheddar with holes, developed by the Nebraska Agricultural Experiment Station in 1940, and named after the local football team.

Cottage Cheese ★

America's favourite cheese next to Cheddar. Americans eat about 2·5kg (5½lb) each per year. Fresh soft white granular cheese made from skimmed milk coagulated with or without rennet. The basic process involves washing the soft curd repeatedly in water to reduce the acid content and then treating it in various ways to produce the many different kinds available. The standard Sweet Curd type is a rennet-curd cheese coated with salted cream and may have large, small or flaked curds. Acid Curd cheese is made without rennet. Country Style uses sour cream. Whipped Cream is coated with whipped cream and has a higher fat content than usual, about 8 per cent. All Cottage Cheese is legally required to have a moisture content of not more than 80 per cent and a fat content of not less than four per cent. Any of the types may be flavoured with fruit or herbs or spices.

Creole

Fresh cows' milk cheese from Louisiana. Traditionally sold as one large curd bathed in thick cream. Particularly popular in New Orleans where homemade versions were once sold on the streets.

Farmer

Fresh white cheese similar to Cottage Cheese.

Gold'n'Rich

Semi-soft buttery Brick-type cheese from the Mid-West. First made in Elgin, Illinois in the 1930s.

Liederkrantz ★   🖧 🌙 50% 🍞 110g (4oz) (

Soft, moist, washed-rind cheese invented by Emil Frey at Monroe, New York in 1892, and now made by the Borden Cheese Company in Van Wert, Ohio. Frey was apparently trying to duplicate the popular Bismarck Schlosskäse then being imported from Germany but which arrived in poor condition after the long Atlantic crossing. The new cheese turned out to be a considerably milder, less pungent form of Limburger. It has a rich velvety golden paste and a very pale brown bacterial crust. It should not be eaten overripe and goes well with beer. The name, meaning 'wreath of song', was that of a singing group to which Frey belonged. It was the Lieder-krantz workers in Ohio who raised a subscription for the repair of Mme Harel's statue in Vimoutiers, France, after it had been destroyed by Allied bombardment in 1944. See *France* (*Camembert*)

Minnesota Slim

Good melting moist loaf developed at the University of Minnesota and dyed bright orange with annatto.

Monterey Jack   🖧 🌙 50% (

Distantly related to Cheddar and first made in Monterey, California in the 1840s. There are two kinds: High Moisture Jack is made from whole milk, ripened for up to six weeks and rather bland and buttery; Dry Jack is a hard tangy grating cheese made from skimmed or partly skimmed milk and ripened for six months or more. Dry Jack is also sold as Grating-Type Monterey. Both cheeses are moulded in various shapes and sizes and sold waxed or vacuum-packed. Dry Jack is often oiled black.

Old Heidelberg   ☆ ⊘ 50% ▱ 110g (4oz) ◖
  Delicate washed rind cheese similar to Liederkrantz and made in Lena, Illinois.

Philadelphia ★
  Brand name of America's best known cream cheese which originated in New York State in the late 19th century. Probably the biggest-selling packaged cheese in the world. Cream cheese and jelly (jam) sandwiches are one of the nation's favourite foods.

Pineapple
  Cheddar, hung to ripen in a net, which produces pineapple shapes and markings. First made in Litchfield, Connecticut in the 1840s. The paste is dry and grainy with a sharp tang. The surface is often treated with shellac making it brown and shiny and even more like a pineapple.

Potted cheese see *Coldpack*

Sno-belle   ☆ ⊘ 50% ⊖ 1kg (2lb) ◖
  Pale soft creamy cheese with white rind flora made from a mixture of whole and skimmed milk. Similar to Camembert but firmer and more buttery with a slight mushroomy flavour.

String Cheese see *Braided Cheese*

Tillamook
  Cheddar from Oregon. Tangy, firm and full-flavoured.

Vermont ★
  Among the best of the American Cheddars. It has a smooth, white sharp paste and a shiny black-waxed rind. Occasionally spiced with caraway or flavoured with sage, which may be real chopped sage or chlorophyll juice extracted from green maize.

CANADA

Given the sizeable French population it is strange that the French appear to have had very little influence on Canadian cheesemaking. French settlers, like the English, brought cheese recipes from home and, in the early days, made cheese in their home dairies. One which became widely known was Fromage Raffiné, a soft cheese still made on a small scale today on the Isle of Orléans. Oka, a fine creamy tangy cheese was invented by a Trappist community near Montreal. Le Moine, a type of Port-Salut, is made at the Abbey of St Benoît du Lac, Brome County and Maigrelet, a semi-soft skimmed milk type, elsewhere in Quebec. But apart from these—all of them rare—the French inventiveness in cheese matters is not particularly evident. Canada is known above all for the excellent Cheddar it produces, two of the best being Black Diamond and Cherry Hill, both ranked by experts alongside the otherwise incomparable English farmhouse cheeses. Made from raw milk, these and most other Canadian Cheddars have escaped the mania for pasteurization which has swept the rest of the continent.

NORWAY see *Scandinavia*. PARAGUAY, PERU see *Latin America*.
POLAND see *Eastern Europe*.

Portugal

Cheesemaking in Portugal is relatively unsophisticated compared with other western European countries. Factory production is a fairly recent phenomenon. In general, mainland cheeses are made of ewes' milk and, to a lesser extent, goats' milk. Cows' milk types are mostly confined to the Azores. A number of foreign cheeses are also made.

Alcobaça   🍖 🥄 55% ⊝ 200g (7oz) 🅳
Serra-type cheese with a very white paste, from Alcobaça.

Azeitão ★   🍖 🥄 45% ⬜ 200–250g (7–9oz) 🅳
Mild, slightly sourish, pale, creamy cheese with a soft, smooth, yellow rind. Coagulated with vegetable rennet (*Cynara cardunculus*) and ripened for three to four weeks. Best eaten in winter and spring. A variant of Serra and of ancient origin, made in Azeitão, a small village near Setúbal.

Cabreiro
Smooth white cheese made in Castelo Branco from mixed ewes' and goats' milk. Eaten fresh or ripened in brine.

Castelo Branco ★   🥄 45% ⊝ 1kg (2lb) 🄲
Made from ewes' or mixed ewes' and goats' milk in Castelo Branco. The paste is white and smooth with a light scattering of small holes. Eaten after three or four weeks' ripening when strong and peppery, or fresh, when it is sold as Queijo Fresco de Castelo Branco.

Castelo de Vide
Serra-type cheese of limited production and variable quality.

Évora ★   · 🥄 45% ⊝ 80–120g (3–4oz) 🄲
Very strong salty cheese made from ewes' milk, occasionally mixed with goats' milk. Yellowy white and crumbly with a darker hard crust. Ripened between six and 12 months and becoming harder with age. From Évora, Alentejo.

Ilha ★   🐄 🥄 45% ⊝ 5–10kg (11–22lb) 🄲
Made in the Azores on the islands of São Miguel, Terceira and Pico (*ilha*, island). A firm-bodied pale yellow cheese with a hard natural crust almost certainly introduced to the islands by English immigrants. The flavour ranges from mild to mellow and nutty depending on age. Ripened between one and three months and eaten up to six months old. Both pasteurized and unpasteurized versions are available.

Nisa
Farm-made Serra-type cheese. Rare and of variable quality.

Pico   🐄 🥄 45% ⊝ 500g (18oz) 🅳
From the island of Pico in the Azores, a pale smooth cheese made from unpasteurized milk. Creamy and fairly piquant. Ripened for three to four weeks. Best in winter and spring.

Queijo Fresco
Fresh, moist, creamy cheese made from any type of milk.

Queijo de Ovelha
Ewes' milk cheese made in Castelo Branco. Coarse and salty.

Queijo Seco
Fresh cheese cured in brine. Greyish, crumbly and salty.

Rabaçal ★   45% ⬜ 1kg (2lb) 🌜
Fresh white curd cheese made from ewes' and goats' milk in the
province of Coimbra. Occasionally ripened for a month or so,
when it becomes firmer and stronger. Often eaten for breakfast
and at the beginning of meals.

Requeijão   🍃 ⊃ ⊜ 100–200g (3½–7oz) ◐
Very mild fresh whey cheese similar to Italian Ricotta, made as
a by-product of ewes' milk cheese production. The whey is
heated to 75°C (167°F), the coagulated solids skimmed off and
then placed in straw baskets to drain. Eaten for breakfast or
before meals. Keeps for a maximum of five days.

Saloio   ⊃ 45% ⊜ 30–50g (1–1¾oz) ◐
Once made from ewes' milk but now increasingly from cows'
milk, a fresh white cheese with a slightly sourish flavour.
Generally available only in restaurants and served before
meals. Made near Lisbon. The name means 'country
bumpkin'.

São Jorge   ⚃ ➤ 45% ⬜ 3–5kg (7–11lb) 🌜
Made on the island of São Jorge in the Azores from
unpasteurized milk. Crumbly with a strong piquant flavour.
Ripened for two to three months. Similar to English Cheddar.

Serpa ★   🍃 ➤ 45% ⊜ 1·7–2kg (3½–4lb) ◐
Variety of Serra, dating back to the Roman occupation. Made
at Serpa, Alentejo, a pale soft to semi-hard cheese with a sharp
peppery flavour. Coagulated with vegetable rennet and
ripened for four to six weeks. A longer ripened version (five
months or more) is sold as Serpa Velho and is very hard and
strong-tasting. Best eaten from December to April.

Serra ★   🍃 ⊃ 45% ⊜ 1·5–2kg (3–4lb) 🌜
Portugal's most famous cheese is an ancient type, farm-made in
the Serra da Estrêla and at Manteigas, Celorico da Beira,
Gouveia, Seia and Guarda. It has a pale yellow buttery paste
with sparse small holes and a soft, smooth, golden rind. The
flavour is mildly lactic and rather refreshing. Coagulated with
vegetable rennet and ripened for four to six weeks. Sometimes
aged further (five months or more) and sold as Serra Velho. Best
between December and April. A harder and inferior factory-
made version is sold as Tipo Serra.

Tomar   🍃 ➤ 45% ⊜ 30–40g (1–1½oz) ◐
Small, firm, tangy cheeses made near Tomar, north-east of
Lisbon. Pale and crumbly with small holes and a tough grey-
yellow crust. Ripened for at least two to three weeks.

Key words

Cabra goat	**Queijo** cheese
Curado ripened	**Seco** dry
Fresco fresh	**Vaca** cow
Ovelha sheep	**Velho** aged

PUERTO RICO see *Latin America*. ROMANIA see *Eastern Europe*. SAUDI
ARABIA see *Middle East*.

Scandinavia

DENMARK

Its temperate climate and predominantly lowland terrain make Denmark an ideal dairying country, yet it has few original cheese types. Nevertheless, Danish cheeses are immensely successful in foreign markets—two-thirds of Danish production is exported to over 100 countries. Most of these cheeses are efficient copies of foreign types which now carry Danish names, thanks to the Stresa Convention of 1951. Some are even displacing similar indigenous cheeses in their country of origin. (Danish Feta, for example, is exported in vast quantities to the Middle East.)

The Danes have always encouraged foreign cheesemakers—the Dutch in the 16th century, the Swiss in the 19th—to share with them their skills and techniques and Hanne Nielsen (see *Havarti*) was indefatigable in her search for new ideas. Nowadays the Danish Ministry of Agriculture sets the highest possible standards of quality control, particularly for exported cheeses. Some would say they go too far in permitting cheese to be made *only* from pasteurized cows' milk. Although milk from other animals can be used, it needs special permission and this has never yet been granted, with the result that there are no Danish ewes' or goats' milk cheeses. Export cheeses must carry the *lurmark* sign (four entwined *lurs*—Bronze Age musical instruments).

Appetitost
Cheese made from cows' milk mixed with sour buttermilk.

Blå Castello ☒ ◐ 70% 150g (5oz) ◖
Recently invented, a cheese with sharply defined dark blue internal veining and a downy white surface mould. Rich and fairly mild, similar to West Germany's Bavaria Blu.

Bolina ☒ ◐ 50% ▭ 3·5kg (8lb) ◖
Like a very mild Gorgonzola with a white, crumbly paste and sparse blue veining.

Danablu ☒ ◐ 50–60% ▭ 3kg (7lb) ◭
Invented in the early 20th century as a substitute for Roquefort and a huge commercial success. Quite different from Roquefort but excellent value and widely available. It can be rather dry and is often very sharp and salty. The paste should be clear and white.

Danbo ☒ ◐ 45% ▱ 6kg (13lb) ◖
A member of the Samsø family, rather bland with a springy pale yellow paste scattered with a few small round holes. The natural rind is firm and butter-coloured but is normally coated with yellow or bright red wax. Usually ripened for about five months and occasionally spiced with caraway seeds.

Elbo ☒ ◐ 40–45% ▱ 6kg (13lb) ◖
A member of the Samsø family, bland, inoffensive and faintly aromatic. Usually coated in red wax.

Esrom ★ ☒ ◐ 45–60% ▱ 1·3kg (3lb) ◖
Washed-rind cheese once known as the Danish Port-Salut but actually closer in character to Tilsit. The paste is pale and

creamy with lots of irregular holes and slits. It has a sweet, rich flavour and a definite spicy aroma when fully aged. Esrom lovers always insist that the rind should definitely be eaten with the cheese.

Fynbo   🎱 ● 45% ⊟ 7kg (15lb) 🐄

A member of the Samsø family, first made on the island of Fyn. Mild, buttery, smooth-textured with a few round holes, usually coated in yellow or red wax. Tropefynbo is smaller, firmer and darker in colour.

Havarti ★   🎱 ● 45% ▱ 4·5kg (10lb) 🐄

Named after the farm owned by Hanne Nielsen, pioneering 19th-century cheesemaker who scoured Europe in search of new techniques and, almost single-handed, revitalized the then moribund Danish cheese industry. Her greatest success was Havarti, once known as Danish Tilsit. It is a supple, creamy, washed-rind cheese with innumerable irregular holes throughout the paste. Fairly full-flavoured at about three months old, it becomes stronger and more pungent with age. The higher-fat version (60 per cent) is richer, slightly softer and may be flavoured with caraway seeds. It has no rind and is usually vacuum-packed in blocks or drums.

Hingino   🎱 ● 32% ⊟ 2kg (4lb) 🎃 🐐

Hard, dry, grating cheese, a modern invention inspired by Italian Canestrato.

Maribo   🎱 ● 45% ⊟ 14kg (31lb) 🐄

Fuller in flavour than Samsø-type cheeses, Maribo has a firmer, drier paste scattered with numerous irregular holes. Ripened for about four months. Usually coated in yellow wax.

Molbo   🎱 ● 45% ○ 2kg (4lb) 🐄

In flavour and appearance almost identical to the red-waxed exported Dutch Edam.

Mycella   🎱 ◗ 50% ▢ 6kg (13lb) 🐄

Once known as Danish Gorgonzola, the veins are greenish-blue and the paste creamy yellow. Mild for a blue cheese.

Rygeost ★

Smoked acid-curd cheese encrusted with caraway seeds. Traditionally eaten around a bonfire on Midsummer's Eve. A naturally smoked cheese, rare nowadays. The fires are kindled from straw, dried grasses or nettles. Served with radishes and beer.

Samsø   🎱 ● 45% ⊟ 14kg (31lb) 🐄

The everyday all-purpose Danish cheese, supposedly inspired by Emmental; it has the holes, though not so many nor so large, but the consistency of the paste is more reminiscent of Cheddar. Like Cheddar it is sold fairly young (about eight to ten weeks old), when it is mild and sweet, or it is aged for several months more to become stronger and more pungent. Named after the island of Samsø and the direct ancestor of many Danish cheese types. See *Danbo, Elbo, Fynbo, Tybo*

Tybo   🎱 ● 40% ▱ 3kg (7lb) 🐐

Smaller and with more holes but virtually identical to Elbo. A caraway-flavoured version is also available.

FINLAND

Lakes and pine forests account for a large part of the land area of Finland and a third of the country lies north of the Arctic Circle so it is surprising to find that dairying is its most important form of agriculture and that it has a well-established cheesemaking tradition. Cheese types that were being made in the Middle Ages are still available today. The techniques used to make some of these traditional cheeses are notably idiosyncratic: the addition of eggs to the curds, for example, and the habit of baking fresh cheeses before an open fire. Such cheeses are mostly farm-made on a small scale but can still be found in specialist stores like the Juustovakka chain of cheese shops. The bulk of Finland's cheese industry is controlled by three co-operatives of which Valio is by far the largest. The most important export cheese is the Finnish version of Emmental, usually sold as 'Finnish Swiss' and considered second only to the Swiss original.

Aura

Strong-tasting, blue-veined, factory-made cows' milk cheese often described in Finland as 'Roquefort'.

Emmental

Not Finnish in origin but the most important cheese in the Finnish dairy industry. It was introduced to Finland in 1856 by a Swiss cheesemaker, Rudolf Klössner, with such success that an 'invasion' of a hundred or more of his fellow-countrymen followed in the years up until the end of World War I. Klössner is said to have started the first batch of Emmental by waving a pine branch over the milk—a branch now on show at the Sippola-Gardens creamery, Finland's oldest cheese factory. Finnish Emmental is made from pasteurized milk. A high-quality product, it is sold at three stages of its maturity: after three months (blue stamp), after six months (red stamp) and after nine months (black stamp). Much of it is exported, especially to the United States.

Ilves see *Munajuusto*

Juhla

The Finnish version of Cheddar.

Juustoleipä ★   40% 250g (9oz)

Rectangular or wheel-shaped fresh cheese made mostly on farms. After coagulating the milk, the cheesemaker drains and presses the curds by hand on to a special wooden plate and then roasts the cheese in front of an open fire. A speciality of central Finland and Lapland, especially Kajaani and Ostrobothnia. The name means 'cheese bread'. Often served for dessert, baked with cream and covered with cloudberries (*lakka*). May be used in coffee instead of milk. Also called Leipäjuusto.

Kappeli

Strong, aromatic, washed-rind cheese similar to German Romadur.

Kesti

Type of Tilsit flavoured with caraway seeds.

Korsholm see *Turunmaa*

Kreivi
Mellow cheese similar to Tilsit.

Kutunjuusto ★ 🔥 🌢 30% 🧀 200g (7oz) 🌙
Rare cheese from Tampere in western Finland. Mild, smooth and fresh, it is made on isolated farms. Unusually made from goats' milk.

Lappi
Similar to Dutch Edam but with a much higher fat content and usually ripened for a longer period.

Leipäjuusto see *Juustoleipä*

Luostari
Semi-hard cows' milk cheese similar to Port-Salut.

Mazurka see *Turunmaa*

Munajuusto ★ 🍳 🌢 40% 😊 1kg (2lb) 🌙
Literally 'egg cheese'. A farmhouse cheese from the south and south-west, made in an unusual way. One or two eggs are added to about six litres of milk, which is then coagulated by heating. After the whey is drained off, the curds are lightly pressed in a wicker basket. The egg yolks give the cheese a wonderful golden colour. There is also a factory version sold under brand names, the best known being Ilves. Like Juustoleipä the fresh cheese can be roasted in front of a fire or grilled. The surface of the cheese becomes speckled with brown and will keep longer than the usual few days.

One of the few countries to specify *actual* fat content as well as dry matter fat content.

Labels are in both Finnish and Swedish

Polar
Very mild hard cheese with large holes.

Salaneuvos
A type of Gouda.

Turunmaa ★ 🌢 50% 😊 6–10kg (13–22lb) 🌙
Originating in the 1500s from the south-west of Finland, a rich, slightly sharp cheese, deliciously creamy and smooth-textured. Almost entirely factory-made. Ripened for two months. Usually eaten for breakfast. The name means 'Turkuland' and derives from Finland's oldest city. Often sold under brand names such as Korsholm and Mazurka.

SCANDINAVIA

ICELAND

Although Iceland's climate is milder than its name suggests
(its shores are washed by the warm waters of the Gulf
Stream), the terrain is not conducive to large-scale dairy
farming. Snowbound volcanic peaks, rivers of solidified lava,
icy glaciers and hot springs make for spectacular scenery but
not for good grazing land. The milk that is produced is
consumed mainly in liquid form—Icelanders drink more per
head than almost anyone else. The residue is made into a
limited number of cheeses, mostly based on other Nordic
types. There are two factory-made 'blues' (*Akureyri, Gradaost*).
Whey cheeses of the Swedish Mesost variety are very
popular, and include a soft, spreadable type (*Mysingur*) and
a harder sliceable one (*Mysuost*). An imitation Swiss
(*Odalsost*) and Edam (*Braudost*) are also widely available, as
are, to a lesser extent, versions of Gouda, Tilsit, Port-Salut,
Camembert and other popular European cheeses.

Sheep flourish in even the hardiest environments and have
been the standby of Icelandic farmers since the island was
first colonized in the 9th century. In the early days they
provided for virtually every need: meat (smoked lamb is still
considered a particular and unique delicacy), clothing and
milk. *Skyr*, Iceland's fresh, white, skimmed-milk cheese, was
traditionally made from ewes' milk though cows' milk is
more often used nowadays. The milk is soured with a starter
consisting of a piece of the previous batch of cheese and then
coagulated with rennet. The rennet used to be obtained by
soaking pieces of vell in whey. The vell also contained traces
of lactic bacteria, including those active in yoghurt-making,
placing Skyr somewhere between a yoghurt and a cheese.
These bacteriological conditions are now reproduced
artificially in the factories where most Skyr is made. It has a
very soft, almost liquid consistency and is consumed in great
quantities usually mixed with milk or cream and sprinkled
with sugar.

NORWAY

Norway is the most mountainous country in Scandinavia.
Coupled with its extraordinarily ragged coastline, deeply
indented with steep-sided fjords, this means that the
proportion of cultivable land is extremely limited and the
potential for good grazing land not much greater. However,
unusually difficult conditions often produce ingenious
responses, which is certainly true of Norwegian cheeses.

Bifost
Mild, white, fresh goats' milk cheese. Also called Hvit Gjetost.

Fjordland
Factory-made block using partly skimmed cows' milk. It has a
pale smooth paste with unevenly distributed large round holes.
Full nutty flavour faintly reminiscent of Emmental.

Gammelost ★   ☼ ➍ 5% ☐ 3kg (7lb) ⓭
'Old cheese'; an ancient type and as intimidating in appearance
as the Vikings who reputedly enjoyed it. It is an excellent
keeping cheese (ideal, perhaps, for long sea voyages) and was
traditionally made in summer for winter use. The pitted hard
brown crust makes it look at least a century old but in fact the

entire making and ripening process takes only a month. Skimmed milk is coagulated with lactic bacteria and heated. The curds are heavily pressed, moulded and then boiled in whey for several hours. The cheeses are left to dry for a day or so and then pierced with *Penicillium*-coated needles or broken up, kneaded with *Penicillium* spores, remoulded and re-pressed. During the ripening period another mould, *Mucor*, grows on the surface, producing a long soft fuzz that is regularly worked back into the cheese by hand. This growth is now artificially induced, although in the past it developed spontaneously from minute traces either left in the moulds from the previous batch of cheese or impregnated in the walls of the dairy. Traditionally the cheeses were stored in straw scented with juniper berries. The result of all this, not surprisingly, is an extremely potent cheese, sharp, strong and aromatic with some blue-green veining in a brownish-yellow paste, quite unique—but an effective antidote for the rigours of a northern winter. Virtually inedible unless sliced very thinly.

Gjetost ★ ◗ 38% ▭ 250–500g (9–18oz) ❻

A whey cheese made from a mixture of cows' and goats' milk or entirely from goats' milk. In the latter case it is marked *Ekte* (genuine) Gjetost. Apart from the milk base the manufacturing process is virtually the same as for Swedish Mesost although the finished product is somewhat darker in colour. Eaten for breakfast, shaved into thin slices, and on spiced fruit cake at Christmas. The appropriate accompaniment is said to be hot coffee or chilled *akevitt*.

Jarlsberg ★ ⏃ ◗ 45% ▱ 10kg (22lb) ● ❻

Based on an old Norwegian type but re-invented in the 1950s and now extremely popular. A good all-purpose cheese with a mellow, slightly sweet flavour and an elastic texture rather similar to Dutch Gouda. The paste is golden yellow with variously sized round holes. Factory-made from pasteurized milk and ripened for six months. A great deal is exported, particularly to the United States.

Knaost see *Pultost*

Mysost

Whey cheese made entirely from cows' milk. See *Gjetost, Sweden* (*Mesost*)

Nøkkelost ⏃ ◗ 45% ▱ 12kg (26½lb) ❻

A milder copy of Dutch Leiden. *Nøkkel* means 'keys', recalling the crossed keys emblem of Leiden cheese.

Norbo ⏃ ◗ 45% ▭ 5kg (11lb) ❻

Recently invented; bland, golden, with holes, yellow rind.

Norvegia ⏃ ◗ 45% ▭ 5kg (11lb) ● ❻

Rindless, vacuum-packed factory product. A very good melting cheese.

Pultost ★

Tangy cows' milk acid-curd cheese ripened for three weeks. Made all over Norway with numerous local variations. Buttermilk, cream and spices (usually caraway seeds) may be added. Also called Knaost or Ramost depending on the particular area.

Ridder   🏵 ➌ 60% ⊟ 2kg (4lb) 🐄
A new variety similar to Saint-Paulin with an orange, lightly washed rind and a rich buttery paste.

SWEDEN

Cheese is eaten a great deal in Sweden, at breakfast time and as part of the ubiquitous *smörgåsbord*. Indigenous types are mostly of the semi-hard, fairly bland variety, though strongly spiced cheeses are also popular. Most interesting of all are the brown whey cheeses—regarded as 'cheese' only by popular consent. Whey cheeses are excluded from most official definitions of cheese since curds form no part of the manufacturing process. These cheeses are not matured in the usual sense yet they cannot be termed 'fresh' since they keep extremely well without refrigeration.

Ädelost   🏵 〰 50% ⊟ 2–3kg (4–7lb) 🐄
An imitation Roquefort made with pasteurized milk. Sharp and salty. Ripened for at least four months.

Billinge
Milder version of Herrgårdsost. Firm, white, with round holes.

Buost
Low-fat, greasy, semi-hard cows' milk cheese from Jämtland.

Drabant
Bland, innocuous type of Herrgårdsost ripened in foil—a good breakfast cheese for fragile constitutions.

Getmesost
Mesost (whey cheese) made with goats' milk whey.

Getost   🐐 ➌ 30% ⊂⊃ 500g (18oz) 🐐
Literally 'goats' cheese', one of the few Swedish cheeses that are still occasionally farm-made. Ripened for a month.

Grevéost   🏵 ➌ 45% ⊟ 14kg (31lb) 🐄
The Swedish version of Emmental, but softer, paler and with huge round eyes. Ripened for about ten months.

Herrgårdsost ★
       🏵 ➌ 30–45% ⊟ 12–18kg (26½–40lb) 🧀 🐄
Literally 'manor cheese' or 'home cheese', once produced on small farms. Originally from West Gotland, it is now factory-made all over Sweden. Basically a Swiss-type, slightly softer than Gruyère with a sparse scattering of small holes, it is a pressed cooked cheese ripened for four to seven months. The rind is usually waxed yellow. The full-fat type (45 per cent, labelled Elite) is made from whole milk. There is also a low-fat version (30 per cent) made from partly skimmed milk and ripened for about four months only.

Hushållsost   🏵 ➌ 30–45% ⊟ 3kg (7lb) 🐄
'Household cheese', one of Sweden's oldest types, smooth, mild and creamy with a faintly acidic edge. The paste is straw-coloured, either with small, round, regular holes or with irregular holes and slits. Sometimes spiced with cumin and cloves. Ripened for one to three months.

Kaggost
Semi-hard, mild cows' milk cheese with a springy creamy yellow paste sometimes spiced with cumin seeds and cloves. Wheel-shaped, ripened for one to three months and mild apart from the spices.

Kryddost ★
'Spiced cheese' a Svecia type spiced with caraway seeds and cloves but matured for several months longer. Traditionally served with crayfish at special parties held during the crayfish season from August 8 onwards.

Lapparnas Renost
Hard smoked cheese from Lapland made with reindeer milk. Extremely rare since reindeers produce very little milk, and seemingly liked only by Lapps, who dunk it in coffee to make it palatable.

Mesost ★   ❦ ● 10–20% ▱ 1–8kg (2–18lb) ❺
'Whey cheese' made by heating whey (a proportion of whole milk, cream or buttermilk is usually added nowadays) to precipitate the residual protein matter. For a whey cheese like Italian Ricotta the process stops at this point. For Mesost the boiling continues until the liquid is reduced considerably and the solids condense into a sticky brown mass caused by caramelization of the milk sugar (lactose). This is then poured into moulds, cooled, cut up into blocks and packed in foil or boxes. Extra sugar and spices are sometimes added. Whey cheese with cream added may be soft and spreadable, but more usually it is firm and close textured, light tan in colour with a bitter-sweet flavour.

Prästost   ❦ ● 50% ⊖ 12–15kg (26½–33lb) ❻
'Priest's cheese', made in Sweden for 200 years. Now mostly factory-made, often from a mixture of pasteurized and unpasteurized milk. Also called Prestost, Saaland Pfarr.

Sveciaost   ❦ ● 30–45% ⊖ 12–16kg (26½–35lb) ❻
'Swedish cheese', the everyday cheese eaten in vast quantities and available in many forms and varying fat contents, spiced or unspiced, young and mild or mature and extremely piquant. These factors are endlessly permutated to produce an extended family of cheeses suiting virtually all tastes.

Västerbottenost   ❦ ● 50% ⊖ 20kg (44lb) ❻
'West Bothnian cheese', invented in the mid-19th century and still exclusively made in West Bothnia. A strong-tasting friable cheese ripened for about a year. Sometimes spiced.

Västgötaost
Hard aromatic cheese from West Gotland.

Keywords

Flødeost (Denmark) cream cheese
Halvfet (Norway) 30 per cent fat
Helfet (Norway) 45 per cent fat
Hytteost (Denmark) cottage cheese

Juusto (Finland) cheese
Kvartfet (Norway) 20 per cent fat
Ost (Denmark, Norway, Sweden) cheese
Ostur (Iceland) cheese

Spain

ATLANTIC OCEAN

AZORES

SPAIN

PORTUGAL

Somebody once said that Africa begins at the Pyrenees.
Certainly Spain often seems like a transitional zone between
that continent and Europe. Apart from Switzerland, Spain is
the highest, most mountainous European country (only
about two-thirds of the land can be said to be productive in
any real sense) but within the overall pattern of plateau and
mountain ranges there are dramatic contrasts in climate and
terrain. Travelling south, the warm, wet, densely wooded
slopes of Galicia and the wild peaks of Asturias and the
Basque provinces give way abruptly to the broad, flat,
intensely arid *meseta*, a high dusty plateau where almost
nothing grows easily. Further south still it becomes bakingly
hot and the landscape looks truly North African with the
esparto covered hills sloping down to the Mediterranean.

118

Ewes' milk cheeses are found all over the country, while cows' milk types are confined to the wetter north and goats' milk cheeses to the mountain ranges. Cheesemaking is relatively uncommercialized. This has some notable advantages: most of the indigenous cheeses are still made from unpasteurized milk by individual farmers in the traditional way, thus retaining their unique qualities. Unfortunately this also means that many of these cheeses are found only in limited quantities and in their particular area of production. As a result, Spanish cheeses are virtually unknown outside Spain which is a pity, for they have an honest, earthy quality closely allied to place, a reminder perhaps of what most cheese was like before machines and marketing men took over.

119

SPAIN

Alicante
🐄 ⏲ 37% ⬡ 150–500g (5–18oz) ◖

Smooth, white, fresh rennet-curd cheese with a clean milky flavour, made in Alicante. The curds are squeezed by hand to drain off some of the excess moisture and pressed into decorative wooden moulds. Eaten fresh.

Aragón
🐑 45% ⬡ 600g–1.5kg (21oz–3lb) ◖

Made from ewes' milk sometimes mixed with goats' milk, this cheese has a firm, very pale paste darkening to golden yellow at the edges with a semi-hard, glossy, butter-coloured rind and a mild, rather pleasant flavour. The curds, coagulated mostly with animal rennet but occasionally with thistle flowers, are shredded and drained by hand and placed in circular dish-shaped wooden moulds. They are then ripened in controlled conditions for about a week. Made in the provinces of Castellón de la Plana and Teruel and also known as Tronchón.

Aralar see *Idiazabal*

Armada
🐄 69% 1.5–3kg (3–7lb) ◖

A curious, very sharp, almost bitter cheese made from beestings. Shaped like a triangular column, the paste is greyish-white, often dry, cracked and crumbly. The rind is hard, yellow and rather oily to touch. The cheese is ripened for about two months. Made in the province of León. Also known as Sobado and Calostro.

Burgos ★
🐑 ⏲ 58% ⬡ 1–2kg (2–4lb) ◖

A fresh rennet-curd cheese made in Burgos. The paste is white, smooth and very mild with just a hint of saltiness. It keeps for about two days after making. Fresh cheeses such as this are often eaten for dessert sprinkled with sugar and honey.

Cabrales ★
🐑 44% ⬡ 1–5kg (2–11lb) ◖

Spain's major veined cheese is made mostly with cows' milk, sometimes mixed with ewes' or goats' milk, on mountain farms in Asturias, mainly around Cabrales and Peñamellera Alta. It is a strong-smelling cheese with a powerful flavour. The paste is an uneven dull white with yellow-brown patches and irregular blue-brown veining. The rind is greyish-red and crusty, sometimes wrapped in sycamore leaves. Ripened in natural limestone caverns for about six months. The term Cabrales can apply generically to goats' milk cheese. Also known as Cabraliego.

Cádiz
🐄 🐑 51% ⬡ 1.5kg (3lb) ◖

Medium-pressed, firm white cheese with an agreeably mellow flavour made in the province of Cádiz. After draining, it is pressed manually into plaited esparto baskets so that its hard golden rind is impressed with the marks of the mould.

Calostro see *Armada*

Camerano
🐄 ⏲ 45% ⬡ 200–800g (7–28oz) ◖

Fresh, white cheese with a mildly acid flavour, basket-moulded and ripened for 24 hours only. Made in the Sierra de Cameros, Logroño. Also called Queso Fresco de Montaña.

Cebrero ★
🐄 🐑 50% 2kg (4lb) ◖

Oddly shaped — a drum with an overhanging rim, like a thick-stalked mushroom — this pressed firm cheese has a creamy close-textured paste and a fairly sharp rustic flavour. The rind is firm and crusty with white streaks radiating from the centre of the 'lid'. It is ripened for three to four days. Made in Lugo in the Cebrero mountains near the Portuguese border and sometimes sold under its Portuguese name Queixo do Cebreiro.

Cervera
67% 1–2kg (2–4lb)

Fresh white cheese rather like Burgos and Villalón, with a milky flavour and the characteristic aroma of sheep's cheese. The shape is variable; more often than not the cheeses are roughly pressed by hand into a lopsided disc. Should be eaten immediately. Made in the Valencia area and also known as Queso Fresco Valenciano.

Estrella see *Oropesa*
Gallego see *Ulloa*

Gamonedo
33% 2–5kg (4–11lb)

Similar to Cabrales, made in the mountain province of Asturias from cows' milk mixed with smaller quantities of ewes' and goats' milk. It has a very lightly veined white paste with many tiny pinpoint holes and a thick, brownish-yellow, coarse dry rind that is sometimes covered with fern fronds. Very strong-smelling with an intensely piquant flavour. Smoked over a period of ten to 20 days and ripened in natural caves for at least two months. Also known as Gamoneu.

Gorbea
45% 500–900g (18oz–2lb)

A piquant pressed cheese with small eyes scattered throughout the creamy yellow paste, which darkens almost to brown at the edges. The rind is very smooth, shiny and unyielding to the touch. Ripened for about a month. Made in Vizcaya.

Grazalema
51% 2–4kg (4–9lb)

Similar to Manchego, a hard-pressed pale yellow cheese with small, variously shaped eyes clustered in the middle of the paste and a striated, golden, oily rind. Has a pleasantly fresh, clean smell and a taste rather like Manchego. Traditionally moulded in esparto baskets although tin moulds are becoming increasingly common. It is doubly salted, first in brine for 48 hours and then buried in a vat of salt for 24 hours before being ripened from two to three weeks up to 90 days. Made in the province of Cádiz at Grazalema.

Idiazabal ★
53% 1–3kg (2–7lb)

Firm, waxy, lightly smoked cheese with small sparse holes from the Basque country. The paste is creamy white and the rind a dark, smooth caramel colour. Ripened for about a month in mountain caves. Has a rather delicate, smoky, herby flavour. Also called Aralar, Urbia and Urbasa.

León
52% 600g–1kg (21oz–2lb)

A mellow cheese with a close-textured white paste and a rough, hard, yellowy rind. Made in Oseja de Sajambre.

Mahón ★
45% 2–4kg (4–9lb)

Made in the Balearic islands, particularly in Menorca. It has a white, creamy, soft paste becoming harder and darker with age. The rind is yellowy brown and hard with darker patches. The cheeses are moulded in cloths, salted in brine and ripened for 20 days or longer, and coated in olive oil.

Málaga
🐐 🥛 58% ⊖ 2kg (4lb) ◐

The most common of several similar goats' milk cheeses made in Andalucía and Extremadura, lightly pressed with a dense creamy white paste and a pleasant typically goaty flavour. The pale, buff-coloured rind shows the impression of the mould. Ripened for five days. Made near Málaga.

Manchego ★
🐑 🥛 50% ⊖ 3kg (7lb) 🧀 ⚫

Spain's most famous cheese is made in the plain of La Mancha. The best Manchego is said to be that from around Ciudad Real, but Toledo, Albacete and Cuenca are also important centres. It is a beautiful cheese, with a firm, ivory to golden paste, sometimes dotted with a few small eyes, and a lovely creamy yellow rind impressed with plaited esparto marks along the sides. The top and bottom mirror the elaborate patterns of the cheese press (where the cheese remains for six to seven hours). During the ripening period, the surfaces become covered with a greenish-black mould that is usually cleaned off before the cheeses are sold, but to satisfy some sections of the market, certain cheeses are sold with the mould coating intact. The taste, depending on the age of the cheese, remains unaltered. Manchego is sold at various stages of its maturity: *fresco* (under three weeks old), *curado* (up to 13 weeks), *viejo* (over three months) and *en aceite* (in olive oil, when it is ripened for at least a year and has a rough blackish rind). Eaten for dessert or grated, when older. Sometimes cubed and fried in olive oil.

Morón
Fresh cheese made of a mixture of cows' and ewes' milk, or sometimes of goats' milk alone. From the town of Morón de la Frontera in the province of Seville. After ripening for 24 hours, it is creamy, white and soft with a clean lactic aroma and mild flavour. May be further aged in a vat of olive oil, after which it is rubbed with paprika. It is then firmer and spicier.

Oropesa
🐑 🥛 46% ⊖ 2kg (4lb) ◐

Similar to Manchego, made in Toledo. Rather darker in colour with a harder, thicker rind. Ripened for about three months and rubbed with olive oil. Also called Queso de la Estrella.

Pasiego prensado
🐄 🥛 49% ⊖ 1–1.5kg (2–3lb) ◐

Made in the Valle de Pas in Santander, usually from whole milk but sometimes from partly skimmed milk mixed with ewes' milk. A pressed cheese with a creamy, mild, white paste and a smooth, shiny, yellow rind. Ripened for one to two weeks.

Pasiego sin prensar
🐄 🌾 8% ⊖ 🧀 ◐

Literally 'unpressed Pasiego', made from cows' milk sometimes mixed with ewes' milk and coagulated with lamb's rennet. Shaped by hand into an irregular disc of variable weight, it has a thick, brownish rind with white powdery streaks. The flavour is mild and milky with slightly sweet overtones. Eaten fresh.

Pata de Mulo see *Villalón*
Patela see *Ulloa*

Pedroches
🐑 🥛 52% ⊖ 2–3kg (4–7lb) ◐

Rich golden, slightly pungent cheese with a hard yellow rind impressed with esparto plaits round the sides. Rather piquant with a touch of saltiness. Ripened for one to two months and then stored in olive oil. Made in the Valle de los Pedroches.

Perilla see *Tetilla*

Plasencia
Semi-hard goats' milk cheese from Extremadura. Pale, creamy paste with a firm golden rind. Rather mellow in flavour. Ripened for a minimum of four months. There is also a smoked version.

Prensado de Orduña   🦋 🌑 49% ⊖ 1.5kg (3lb) 🅾
Pressed cheese with a firm, smooth, glossy, golden rind and a buttery, yellow, piquant paste studded with tiny eyes. Ripened for a month. Made in the Sierra de Guibijo in Alava.

Puzol   🦋 🌙 50% ⊖ 300g–2kg (10oz–4lb) 🅾
Fresh, mild white cheese which should be eaten within two days. Made in Puzol in the province of Valencia. Also called Queso Fresco Valenciano.

Queso Añejo de Cabra de la Sierra de Huelva
🐐 🌑 52% ⊖ 1kg (2lb) 🅾
Lightly pressed cheese with a dark orangey paste and a rough brownish rind. Very piquant with a penetrating aroma. Eaten fresh or ripened for about three months. Made in the Sierra de Aracena and the Sierra de Andévalo. Also called Queso de Cabra Sudado, Queso de Cabra Curado and Queso de Cabra Picón.

Queso de la Estrella see *Oropesa*
Queso Fresco de Montaña see *Camerano*
Queso Fresco Valenciano see *Cervera*, *Puzol*

Queso do los Montes San Benito de Huelva
🦋 🌑 51% ⊖ 🅾
A hard-pressed cheese, coagulated with vegetable rennet, with a smooth, dry, tawny-coloured rind and a buttery paste. Ripened for three weeks and eaten up to two months afterwards, or, if stored in olive oil, for two years. Made in the south-west in the province of Huelva. Also called Queso de Oveja de Andévalo.

Queso de Oveja de Andévalo see *Queso do los Montes*

Quesucos   🌑 46% ⊖ 100g–3kg (3½oz–7lb) 🅾
Small- to medium-sized unpressed cheeses made from various milks in the province of Santander. Usually mild in flavour, sometimes smoked, mostly produced in summer.

Roncal   🦋 🌑 43% ▢ 2kg (4lb) 🌑 🅱
Piquant, slightly greenish cheese with a hard, leathery rind formed by salting, washing and smoking. Ripened for one to two months. Made in Roncal, Navarre. Good for grating.

San Simón   🌀 🌑 40% 1–2kg (2–4lb) 🌙
Smoked pear-shaped cheese from Lugo with a creamy paste, a glossy chestnut-coloured rind and a mildly acid flavour.

Serena   🦋 🌑 52% ⊖ 1kg (2lb) 🅾
Cheese rather like Pedroches, coagulated with vegetable rennet and moulded in esparto hoops. The paste is rich and yellowy with numerous variously sized holes. Made in Badajoz.

Sobado see *Armada*

Soria 🐐 🌑 55% 500g–1kg (18oz–2lb) ◗
Smooth, white, fresh cheese similar to Camerano but with a slightly darker, firmer crust and a saltier flavour. Moulded in wicker baskets. From Soria.

Tetilla ⚱ 🌑 40% 1kg (2lb) ◖
A flattish pear-shaped cheese with a pleasantly clean, slightly sourish, salty flavour. Made in Pontevedra, La Coruña and Lugo. Also called Perilla.

Torta del Casar 🐑 🌑 57% ⊖ 1kg (2lb) ◗
A quick-ripening cheese made mostly in the spring around the old Roman town of Cáceres near the Portuguese border. The cheese has a soft, rich, creamy, golden paste and a dry, darker rind and is best eaten when the rind becomes cracked and streaky. It is coagulated with vegetable rennet and ripened for two to three weeks.

Tronchón see *Aragon*

Tudela
Ewes' milk cheese similar to Manchego. From Navarre.

Ulloa ⚱ 🌑 45% ⊖ 1kg (2lb) ◖
A mild cheese with a white paste and a springy yellow rind. The curds are scooped into cheese cloths, moulded and lightly pressed before being ripened. Made in the provinces of La Coruña, Lugo and Pontevedra. Also called Gallego and Patela.

Urbasa, Urbia see *Idiazabal*

Valdeteja 🐐 🌒 72% ⊖ 1kg (2lb) ◗
Fairly sharp, white cheese with a pronounced goaty smell. The rind is dry, crusty and yellow-orange in colour. It is ripened for two to three weeks. Made at Valdeteja in León.

Veyos 🌒 51% ⬚ 500g (18oz) ◗
This strong white cheese is made from ewes' or goats' milk or a mixture of the two, and has a rough grey-brown rind. It is lightly smoked during the ripening period, which lasts from one to four weeks. Made in Comarca de los Veyos in Asturias. Also called Veyusco.

Villalón ★ 🐑 🌒 54% ⬭ 500g–2.5kg (18oz–5½lb) ◖
Fresh, white, mild, slightly sour cheese, hand-pressed and steeped in brine for two to three hours, usually eaten immediately, but occasionally ripened for longer periods. From Villalón de Campos, Valladolid. Also called Pata de Mulo.

Key words	
Anejo aged	**Oveja** ewe
Blando soft	**Picón** piquant
Cabra goat	**Prensado** pressed
Curado medium-ripened	**Queso** cheese
Duro hard	**Suave** mild
En aceite in olive oil	**Vaca** cow
Fresco fresh	**Viejo** mature

SWEDEN see *Scandinavia*.

Switzerland

The Swiss once used cheese as currency. Artisans, workers and priests in the Middle Ages were paid partly in cash and partly in fine Swiss cheeses—a form of coinage that could not be debased nor depreciate with time. Early exports were, no doubt, based on the same bartering principles. Cheeses were taken over the Alps into Italy and exchanged for rice, spices and wine. This eminently civilized form of trade has now gone but the Swiss still place a justifiably high value on their own cheeses, which were recognized as particularly superb even in Roman times. The climate, the richness of the milk and, above all, fine cheesemaking skills transmitted from generation to generation have all contributed to the generally excellent quality of Swiss cheese. The Swiss have also been especially inventive in their cheese cookery. Apart from the famous *fondue* and *raclette*, they make marvellous cheese soups, puddings and soufflés and splendid huge cheese tarts, *Käsewahe*.

Agrini
Small, soft, cylindrical Ticinese goats' milk cheeses with white rind flora.

Alpkäse
Generic term for hard or semi-hard mountain cheeses. Mostly wheel-shaped with tough dry rinds and a variety of holes. There are innumerable regional variations such as Berner, Bündner, Innerschweizer, Tessiner and so on.

Anniviers see *Raclette*

Appenzell(er) ★   50%   6–8kg (13–18lb)
Delicate cheese with a fine, fruity flavour, made from un-pasteurized milk. The paste is smooth and dense, scattered with a few pea-sized, perfectly round holes. The rind, washed with

spices and white wine or cider, is hard and thick. Ripened for four to six months. Originated in the canton of Appenzell in the 8th or 9th century. See *Rasskäse*

Avers
Soft white goats' milk cheese with a lightly bloomy skin.

Bagnes see *Raclette*

Bellelay see *Tête de Moine*

Bergkäse
Generic term for hard or semi-hard mountain cheeses.

Berner Alpkäse
Hard wheel-shaped cows' milk cheese from the Bernese alps.

Binn see *Raclette*

Blenio
Made in Ticino. A kind of Gruyère.

Bratkäse   45%   1–1·6kg (2–3lb)
Grilling cheese similar to Raclette but usually eaten with bread. Made from pasteurized or unpasteurized milk, it has a rich buttery yellow paste with many variously sized holes and a bright orange, firm, dry rind. Ripened between six and ten weeks. These cheeses were traditionally roasted on the end of a stick over an open fire. The best are said to be those from Nidwalden and Obwalden.

Brienzer Mutschli
Semi-hard cows' milk cheese made in the Bernese alps.

Bündner Alpkäse
Thick, wheel-shaped, hard cows' milk cheese with many cherry-sized holes. Made in Grisons.

Chascöl d'Alp
Made in Grisons, a hard wheel-shaped cheese made from cows' milk. Chascöl da Chascharia is a skimmed milk version of the same cheese. Chascöl Chevra is made from goats' milk.

Chaux d'Abel   45%   6–8kg (13–18lb)
Smooth, sweetish, pale yellow cheese with a few irregular holes and an orange, firm, dry rind. Made near Neuchâtel.

Conches see *Raclette*

Convive
Small, soft, rich cows' milk cheese with white rind flora.

Emmental(er) ★   45% 60–130kg (132–286lb)
Commonly known throughout the world as 'Swiss' cheese and imitated in many other countries, Emmental accounts for over half of Swiss cheese production. Genuine Swiss Emmental (stamped 'Switzerland' all over the rind) is made only from unpasteurized milk in both farms and factories. It is a pressed cooked cheese instantly recognizable by the round walnut-sized holes evenly distributed throughout the firm dense golden paste. The name comes from the Emmen valley near Bern

where it originated. It takes about 1,000 litres of milk (the average daily yield of 80 cows) to make one 80kg (176lb) cheese. Evening and morning milk are mixed and coagulated with rennet. At the same time a culture of propionic acid producing bacteria is added to the milk. The curds are cut with a cheese harp, shredded into minute pieces, then 'cooked' in the whey for about half an hour. The mass of curd is then wrapped in a cheesecloth and lifted into a wooden hoop to drain. It is turned and pressed several times, soaked in a brine bath for one or two days and then taken to special cellars for ripening. It is during this ripening period of between four and ten months that the famous holes are formed. A secondary fermentation takes place after the curds have firmed and bubbles of gas become trapped in the mass. The number, size and shape of the holes depend on a host of factors: the scalding temperature of the curds, the level of salting, the temperature and humidity of the ripening store, the length of ripening, the number of times the cheese is turned during the ripening and so forth. The precise level of all these factors is itself determined by the way each batch of curds is 'working'—something that can only be judged by expert cheesemakers with years of experience. It is not surprising therefore that Emmental is generally considered to be one of the most difficult cheeses to make successfully, nor that the Swiss, with their centuries of experience, remain unimpressed by their innumerable would-be competitors elsewhere. 'Anyone can make the holes,' they say, 'but only the Swiss can make the cheese.'

Etivaz see *Shrinz*
Fribourg see *Vacherin Fribourgeois*
Fromage de Chalet see *Spycher*

Frutigtal
Hard cows' milk cheese made in the Bernese alps.

Gaiskäsli see *Germany, Federal Republic*
Gessenay see *Shrinz*
Glarnerkäse see *Sapsago*
Gomser see *Raclette*
Grüner Käse, Grüner Kräutkäse see *Sapsago*

Gruyère ★   45%   20–45kg (44–99lb)

Like Emmental, a pressed cooked cheese, although Gruyère wheels are much smaller and have straight rather than convex sides. The holes are also smaller, roughly pea-sized, and much more sparsely scattered through the paste. The rind is a coarse reddish brown stamped all over with the word 'Switzerland' to indicate a genuine Swiss product. For Gruyère the curds are cut less finely, scalded at a higher temperature, pressed harder and longer and ripened at a lower temperature but for the same period (four to ten months), producing a drier, firmer cheese with a more pronounced sweetish flavour and a typically nutty aroma. A particularly fine cheese is marked by a slight dampness in the eyes and fine slits just beneath the rind. Gruyère is an excellent cooking cheese (even better than Emmental). Sauce Mornay is based on it, as is *fondue*, a hot cheese dip flavoured with garlic, pepper, white wine, kirsch and lemon juice, traditionally accompanied by more kirsch or a glass of hot tea. Gruyère, which originated in the town of the same name in the 12th century, should be kept wrapped in a cloth dampened with salt water.

Hasliberg
Hard cows' milk cheese made in the Bernese alps.

Haudères, Heida see *Raclette*
Hobelkäse see *Sbrinz*
Illiez see *Raclette*
Innerschweizer see *Alpkäse*
Justistal see *Sbrinz*
Kräuterkäse see *Sapsago*

Maggia
Hard unpasteurized cows' milk cheese made in Ticino.

Mutschli   🐄 ● 45% ▭ 500g–5kg (18oz–11lb) €
Originally a mountain cheese now made all over Switzerland from pasteurized and unpasteurized milk. Fragrant, sweet-tasting with irregular holes and a warm, slightly rough, golden crust.

Nidelchäs
Soft creamy cows' milk cheese with a white bloomy rind. Shaped like a thick disc.

Nidwaldner Bratkäse, Obwaldner Bratkäse see *Bratkäse*
Orsières see *Raclette*

Paglia
Creamy blue-veined cheese similar to Gorgonzola. Ripened on beds of straw. Made in Ticino.

Piora ★   🐄 ● 45% ◒ 8–16kg (18–35lb) ◑
Delicate rich cheese with many small holes. Made in Ticino. Vero Piora is made on the Alp Piora itself; Tipo Piora is made on other mountains in the same area; Uso Piora is made from a mixture of cows' and goats' milk. All are ripened for about six months.

Raclette ★   🐄 ● 50% ◒ 5–7kg (11–15lb) ● 6
Literally 'scraper', the name given to a family of semi-hard cheeses mostly from the canton of Valais. A firm, buttery cheese made from unpasteurized milk, it has a golden paste with a few small holes and a rough grey-brown rind deeply impressed with the name of the cheese. The flavour is full and fruity and similar to Gruyère. Eaten as it is or particularly suitable for use in the traditional Swiss dish also called *raclette*. To make raclette a whole cheese is sliced in half and the cut surface placed before an open fire. As the cheese melts it is scraped on to a dish and eaten immediately with potatoes boiled in their skins, pickled onions and gherkins. There are many types of Raclette cheese. Among those officially recognized as the best are Anniviers, Bagnes, Binn, Conches, Gomser, Haudères, Heida, Illiez, Orsières, Simplon and Walliser.

Rahm-Käsli
Small cows' milk cream cheeses with white rind flora. Often oval-shaped. Fat content 55 per cent.

Rasskäse
A type of Appenzell made with skimmed milk, giving it a very low fat content of around 16 per cent. Much darker, sharper and more pungent than ordinary Appenzell.

Royalp ♨ ➌ 45% ⊖ 4–5kg (9–11lb) ⓫

Introduced in the 19th century by German cheesemakers and known as Tilsit in Switzerland and Royalp abroad. More like Appenzell than German Tilsit, it is firmer with far fewer more regularly shaped holes. It has a rather mild flavour with a spicy, piquant aftertaste. The unpasteurized version, made only in eastern Switzerland where the cheese originated, is marked with a red label. The pasteurized version, made all over the country, has a green label.

Printed in red on the rind or on the package are the mark of the Swiss Cheese Union and the word 'Switzerland'.

These both guarantee the authenticity of exported Gruyère, Emmental, Sbrinz, Royalp and Appenzell

Saanen ♨ ➌ 40–45% ⊖ 15–30kg (33–66lb) ⓫ ◖

Made in the Saanen valley in the Bernese Oberland since the 16th century. A very hard cheese similar to an Italian Grana, it has a deep yellow brittle paste with many tiny pinpoint holes and is used mostly for grating. Generally ripened for two to three years but will keep indefinitely.

Sapsago ♨ ➌ 3% ▭ 100–200g (3½–7oz) ⓫ ⓫

A cheese with many names and few uses: Glarnerkäse, Grüner Käse, Grüner Kräuterkäse, Kräuterkäse, Schabziger, or simply 'Green Cheese'. Whatever the name, it is a rock hard, pale green cheese, shaped like a cylinder tapering slightly at the top, strong and spicy to taste. Made of skimmed milk or whey, sometimes mixed with buttermilk, heated with lactic acid or vinegar to precipitate the proteins. The solids are then heavily pressed, ground up and mixed with powdered herbs and pressed again into special moulds to produce the characteristic shape known as 'Stöckli'. It was introduced into the canton of Glarus by monks at least 500 years ago. The curious flavour comes from blue melilot (*Melilotis coerulea*), a herb brought back from Asia Minor by crusaders and still found in the area in which the cheese is made. Sapsago is a condiment cheese, used only for grating. It is sprinkled on bread or on local dishes. Sold wrapped in foil or powdered in cartons.

Sbrinz ★ ♨ ➌ 45% ⊖ 20–45kg (44–99lb) ⓫ ⓫

Probably the cheese that Pliny knew as *caseus helveticus*, 'Swiss cheese'. Sbrinz is the most ancient of Swiss cheeses and there has been a vigorous Italian market in it for many centuries. It is generically related to Italian Grana cheese, being a long-ripened, extra-hard, pressed, cooked cheese used mostly for grating and very spicy and piquant in flavour. Similarly, it is said to be easily digestible and has some reputation as a medicament. Made only from unpasteurized milk and only in Central Switzerland: in Lucerne, Unterwalden, Schwyz and Zug. The name derives from the village of Brienz in the Bernese Oberland. It is ripened (stored, unusually, on edge) for 18 months to three years. Young sliceable Sbrinz is sold as Spalen or Spalen Schnittkäse. In Ticino it may appear as Sulle Spalle, reflecting in the local dialect how such cheeses were once transported on muleback through the St. Gotthard Pass. It is an excellent grating cheese and also melts extremely well, making it ideal for cooking. It is frequently also eaten as an appetizer, shaved into paper-thin curly slivers (*rebibes*). In this form it (and other hard cheeses similarly treated) is sometimes referred to as Hobelkäse (from *Hobel*, a carpenter's plane). Sbrinz is the best known (and the best) of a large family of extra-hard cows' milk cheeses. Other reputable members include Etivaz, Gessenay, Justistal and Splügen.

Schabziger see *Sapsago*

Schwyzer
Hard cows' milk cheese made in Central Switzerland either in the mountains (*fromage d'alpage*) or the valleys (*fromage de campagne*).

Sedrun
Semi-hard wheel-shaped goats' milk cheese with a thick dry greyish crust. Ripened for a maximum of five months. Dry matter fat content is 45 per cent.

Sérac
Fresh whey cheese similar to Italian Ricotta. Occasionally ripened or smoked or seasoned with herbs and spices. Fat content is usually at least 15 per cent.

Séré 125–500g (4–18oz)
Fresh cheese made from whole or skimmed pasteurized milk. There are three types: *maigre* (0–15 per cent fat), *gras* (40 per cent fat), *à la crème* (50 per cent fat).

Simplon see *Raclette*
Spalen (Schnittkäse), Sulle Spalle see *Sbrinz*
Splügen see *Sbrinz*

Spycher
Low fat, semi-hard, drum-shaped smooth yellow cows' milk cheese with a soft brown rind. Also called Fromage de Chalet.

Tessiner see *Alpkäse*

Tête de Moine ★ 50% 500g–2kg (18oz–4lb)
A monastic cheese made only from summer milk and available in winter. The season lasts from September until March (traditionally the cheeses go on sale each year when the first leaves of autumn begin to fall). It is a delicate, creamy, pressed, uncooked cheese ripened for four to six months in cool cellars. The paste is straw yellow and the rind rough and rather greasy to touch. It was invented by monks at Bellelay Abbey who later taught the method to local farmers. The name (meaning 'monk's head') derives, some say, from a tax levied by the abbey whereby the farmers would provide one cheese for each monk during the season. Others say it refers to the tonsured appearance of the cheese when it is served in the traditional way: with the top sliced off and the rind cut away to a depth of about 2cm (¾in) all round. The cheese is usually sliced into thin curls with a special knife and eaten sprinkled with pepper and powdered cumin. Also called Bellelay.

Tilsit Suisse see *Royalp*

Toggenburger Ploderkäse

💠 ➌ 15% ⬭ 7–13kg (15–29lb) €

Made in the Alps north of the Walensee, a cube-shaped white-pasted cheese made from skimmed milk coagulated by lactic fermentation. It is Switzerland's only sour milk cheese. The milk is usually soured naturally, then heated and the curds allowed to drain in the moulds without pressing. During the six month ripening period the cheeses become covered with a fat layer (*Speckschicht*) – not actually fat but a thick bacterial smear which is often removed before the cheeses are sold.

Tomme Vaudoise 💠 ➋ 45% ⬭ 100–170g (3½–6oz) €

From the canton of Vaud, north of Lake Geneva, small quick-ripened cheeses made mostly in small dairies from pasteurized or unpasteurized milk. The paste is rich yellow and supple with a lightly crumpled covering of white mould which becomes streaked with red as the cheeses mature. Very mild, faintly spicy and sometimes flavoured with cumin. Ripened for about a week.

Urner

Low-fat hard cows' milk cheese from Central Switzerland.

Vacherin Fribourgeois

💠 ➌ 45% ⬭ 6–10kg (13–22lb) ● 🐄

Quite a different cheese from Vacherin Mont d'Or but often confused with it. This is a mountain cheese, one of the oldest in Switzerland, dating back to the 15th century. Made only in the canton of Fribourg from pasteurized or unpasteurized milk. Smaller and softer than Gruyère, it has a dull yellow paste with many small holes and slits. The rind is pinkish brown and rather coarse. There are two kinds: Vacherin à Fondue is winter-made from a mixture of whole or skimmed milk and is used mainly in *fondue fribourgeoise* or *fondue moitié-moitié*, mixed half and half with Gruyère; Vacherin à la Main is softer, maturing after about three months and is used mainly as a dessert cheese.

Vacherin Mont d'Or ★

💠 ➋ 50% ⬭ 200g–3kg (7oz–7lb) 🐄

Justly famous, a marvellous cheese when at its best, it has a rich velvety texture and a faintly resinous flavour. Made in the Vallée de Joux near the French border from unpasteurized milk and virtually identical to the French cheese of the same name. It is a winter cheese, bound with a strip of pine bark and sold in wooden boxes (in which it is also customarily served). The paste is a dull, almost greeny yellow and has the consistency of thick clotted cream. The crust, pale reddish brown rather like lightly baked bread, becomes gently crumpled when the cheese is *à point*. Served traditionally, this crust is removed in one piece and the inside scooped out with a spoon. If the cheese is sliced, the cut surfaces should be protected with a small sheet of glass or wood to prevent the paste flowing out of the crust. A whole Vacherin Mont d'Or makes a wonderfully luxurious dessert cheese. Locally it is also eaten sprinkled with cumin seeds and accompanied by plain boiled potatoes.

Walliser see *Raclette*

SYRIA, TURKEY see *Middle East*. TUNISIA see *Africa*. UNITED STATES see *North America*.

USSR

Some interesting indigenous cheeses come from the European fringes of Russia, from Trans-Caucasia (especially Armenia, home of early cheesemaking) and from the mountain ranges along the Chinese and Mongolian borders. Few of these cheeses reach the West. The Russian for cheese is Sir (Сыр).

Altaysky (Алтайский)

🐄 ➤ 40% ⊖ 12–20kg (26½–44lb) 🍎 ◖

Hard-pressed cooked cheese with holes, similar to Emmental.

Daralagyazhsky (Даралагяжский)

Semi-hard Armenian cheese made from ewes' or goats' milk.

Desertny Bely 🐄 ➤ 50% ⊖ 500g (18oz) ◖
(Десертный Белый)

Factory-made cheese with white rind flora ripened for a week.

Dorogobuzhsky 🐄 ➤ 45% ⊏ 500g (18oz) ◖
(Дорогобужский)

Oily, spreadable cheese with a damp reddish rind. Ripened for about six weeks. Piquant and strong-smelling.

Estonsky (Эстонский) 🐄 ➤ 45% ⊡ 2–3kg (4–7lb) ◖

Hard mild cheese with a waxed rind. Ripened for one month.

Gornoaltaysky ★ ➤ 50% ⊡ 10–15kg (22–33lb) 🍎 ◖ ◖
(Горноалтайский)

Strong grating cheese made from ewes' or cows' milk and ripened for three months. Occasionally smoked.

Kostromskoy 🐄 ➤ 45% ⊖ 5–12kg (11–26½lb) ◖
(Костромской)

Mild factory-made dessert cheese with a red waxed rind.

Latviysky (Латвийский) 🐄 ➤ 45% ⊏ 2kg (4lb) ◖

Strong, smelly, washed-rind cheese ripened for two months.

Moskovsky (Московский)

Hard-pressed cows' milk cheese ripened for four months.

Motal (Мотал)

White, brined ewes' or cows' milk cheese, farm-made in the Caucasus and ripened for about three months.

Sirok (Сырок)

Acid- or rennet-curd cheese made from cows' milk.

Sovetsky (Советский) 🐄 ➤ 50% ▽ 12–16kg (26½–35lb) ◖

Piquant rather rubbery cheese with holes made in the Altai mountains and ripened for about four months.

Stepnoy (Степной)

Greasy cows' milk cheese much the same as East German Steppenkäse. Strong, sometimes spiced with caraway.

Yerevansky (Ереванский) ★

Named after the capital of Armenia, a semi-hard, white, brined cheese made from ewes' milk. Ripened in tins.

VENEZUELA see *Latin America*. YUGOSLAVIA see *Eastern Europe*.

Buying, serving and storing cheese

All cheeses are temperamental to a greater or lesser extent and, however fine, can be ruined by careless handling. One might almost say that the finer the cheese, the more it needs cosseting. Processed cheese is virtually indestructible—a measure perhaps of its awfulness. Since cheese is a relatively expensive commodity, care in buying, serving and storing it makes sound economic sense as well as being gastronomically rewarding.

Buying cheese

The first essential is to find a reputable cheesemonger, where you can find a wide selection of cheeses in excellent condition from which to choose with confidence. There are, of course, countless places where cheese is sold and experience alone will teach you which are the best. A wide selection, although important, is not the only criterion. A few well-chosen cheeses displayed with care and attention to their particular characteristics may well be a better indication of a good shop than a huge indiscriminate array. Many shops unfortunately stock far too many cheeses without having the turnover to justify it and cheeses left on the shelf for too long will inevitably deteriorate. A shop where you are allowed, even encouraged, to taste before you buy is almost bound to be a good one. It shows that the retailer has every confidence in his own product.

An old port trade saying advises: *'Buy on an apple, sell on cheese.'* This is because cheese brings out the best in the wine, whereas the sharpness of an apple brings out any faults.

Unless you are prepared to place yourself entirely in the hands of your cheesemonger, you will need to know something about the desirable and undesirable features of each cheese. Some guidelines have been given in the listings in this book. The nature of the paste, the rind, the eyes or the veins all hold clues to the condition of a particular cheese. Examine the label if there is one. Many cheeses are now subject to legal protection and most countries have stringent rules concerning the labelling of food products generally. The presence or absence of information can tell you a great deal about the origins, authenticity and composition of a cheese: for example, whether it is farmhouse- or factory-made, pasteurized or unpasteurized, the fat content, the type of milk and so on. Many cheese labels are small masterpieces in their own right. (Some examples of labels from various countries can be seen elsewhere in this book.)

Remember that it is nearly always better to buy pieces cut from a whole cheese rather than pre-packed sections. Cheese should always be cut properly, either with a wire cutter or a special knife, and then be covered with cling-film or metal foil.

Serving cheese

The first great bone of contention is when during a meal the cheese should be served. The French, in particular, express great horror at any departure from their normal practice, which is to serve the cheese after the salad and before the dessert. But every country has its own favoured ritual. In some countries, such as Greece, sliced cheese is served with a meal as a side dish and can be eaten at any time. Cheese is served for breakfast in Germany, the Netherlands and Scandinavia and in many Middle Eastern countries. In Portugal cheese is frequently eaten before the main meal as an appetizer. There are usually good reasons for such habits, deriving in part from the nature of each country's cheeses. Then there are favoured combinations of cheese with other foods (apple pie and Wensleydale, pears and Gorgonzola, radishes and Rygeost, and so on). The enjoyment of cheeses can be influenced as much by *how* they are served as with what and when. Some demand to be spread, others spooned, others sliced very thinly. Some cheeses (generally fresh ones) are not usually served as part of a cheese board. but are eaten separately, served in different ways. Some are used only or mostly for cooking.

Storing cheese

If possible, avoid the problem of storage altogether and buy only as much cheese as you can eat on that day or the next. Most good cheesemongers are better equipped to store cheese properly than the average household. Few of us can afford the luxury of a cheese cellar, and the old-fashioned larder or pantry—an excellent short-term cheese store—has been replaced by refrigerators and freezers. On the whole these do nothing for cheese, although fresh cheeses must be kept in the refrigerator. Soft cheeses (Brie, Camembert, etc.) can be stored for a day or so in the warmest part of the refrigerator (the vegetable drawer is best). Semihard and hard cheeses should be stored in a cool cupboard for preference. Cheeses should always be wrapped closely and separately (to avoid mingling flavours). Cling-film or foil is ideal in most cases, but some cheeses (Granas, for example) are better wrapped in a damp cloth. All cheeses, even fresh ones, need to be taken out of the refrigerator or cupboard some time before being served (up to an hour for soft cheeses, longer for hard ones) in order to develop their flavour to the full. Be extra careful with soft cheeses: they are apt to liquefy if kept in a warm room for too long. Hard cheeses under the same conditions tend to become harder and may sweat. Serve only as much cheese as is likely to be eaten at any one time, to avoid returning it to the cold store: cheeses do not take kindly to frequent oscillations of temperature. Finally, in spite of the recommendations of many manufacturers, never put cheese in the freezer. It is one sure way of destroying its flavour and texture irretrievably.

Man has yet to find a better companion to cheese than wine.

Pierre Androuet THE ENCYCLOPEDIA OF CHEESE

What to drink with your cheese

The words cheese and wine are firmly associated in the public mind, and like vodka and caviar are bracketed as perfect partners.

Sadly it is not always so simple. There are so many cheeses and too many wines to choose from. And you cannot mix all the cheeses with all of the wines. The choice is worth a little consideration. First decide what takes priority, the cheese or the wine: are the cheeses very special, or is the wine a great one to be sipped rather than quaffed? If the cheese is the important partner, choose wine to match either its character or its birthplace. Strong, pungent cheeses require young, full-bodied red wines or a sweet white wine. Soft cheeses, and those of finer taste, call for more quality and age in the wine. Fine wines need a restrained partner. Often, both wine and cheese will be ordinary, which makes the choice easier and perhaps more interesting. Some combinations are suggested in the table below.

Wine country often produces cheese, making local partnerships an intriguing possibility. Stick to the humbler wines, the *vin de pays*, the Italian country wines. Great wines, even from a cheese district, somehow have less in common with local food than the small wines destined for everyday drinking. Origin-matching often falls down outside the wine-making zone, where the local beverage may be beer and cider, especially the traditional sorts. The cheeses of England and Normandy marry well with their local drinks.

Experiment with mild cheeses and the lesser known varieties. Try sweet wines with the fattier cheeses, sharp whites with Fromage Frais. The only real rule is to take account of quality. It is disappointing to pay through the nose for good wine and then to drink it with a pungent cheese that takes over the palate and every other sense.

Think twice before falling for the classic combination of Blue Stilton and vintage port. Good port—when it is to be found—is an experience that needs no complement. The same goes for a decent Stilton. Drink port with Stilton by all means, but choose a relatively young tawny, a good ruby or a late-bottled kind. The cheese needs the sweetness and strength a fortified wine brings, but can somehow overbalance the delicate structure of a fine vintage port.

Finally, if you do not or cannot drink alcohol, be warned. Never drink water with cheese: the combination is utterly indigestible.

Appenzell	light fruity reds, Merlot, Beaujolais
Asiago	lively full-bodied Piedmontese reds
Banon	dry delicate Provençal whites, reds or rosés, Cassis, Gigondas, Côtes de Provence, Chinon
Bel Paese	light rosés, Valpolicella, Barbera, Chianti
Bleu d'Auvergne	Saint Pourçain, Cornas, Châteauneuf-du-Pape
Blue Cheshire	reds from Burgundy or the Médoc, Australian reds, Chilean Cabernet, port
Blue Stilton	tawny port, good amontillado sherry, Dão, red Rioja, Barolo, Hermitage
Blue Wensleydale	St-Emilion, lesser Médocs
Bondon	Touraine Sauvignon, (Normandy) cider
Brick	full fruity reds, beer
Brie	Sancerre, Frascati, Médoc, Bordeaux reds, Côtes du Roussillon

Brinza	beer
Caciotta	Chianti
Camembert	white Burgundy, Rhine whites, claret
Cantal	Gaillac red, Chinon
Cheddar	any red wine—the better the Cheddar the better the wine—Burgundies, Châteauneuf-du-Pape, Barolo, Zinfandel, tawny ports, beer, real ale
Cheshire	Beaujolais Villages, Loire Gamay
Chèvre	French country reds
Coulommiers	Nuits-St-Georges
Crottin	Sancerre, Chablis
Danablu	full-bodied reds, clarets, Burgundies, Rhône reds, Rioja
Edam	light fruity reds or whites, beer
Emmental	fruity reds or whites, Nierstein, Bourgogne-Mâcon, Champigny, Fendant
Esrom	any light to solid red depending on age of cheese
Feta	dry Greek whites, retsina, ouzo
Fontina	Merlot, Pinot Grigio
Fourme d'Ambert	Condrieu
Friese Nagelkaas	beer, whisky
Fromage Frais	Soave, Anjou Blanc, Vinho Verde
Gammelost	strong reds
Gaperon	Corbières
Gjetost	strong black coffee, akevitt
Gorgonzola	Barbera, Barolo, robust Sardinian or Provençal reds
Gouda	Beaujolais Villages for young cheeses, full-bodied reds for mature ones, beer
Gruyère	Rhône white or red, light fruity Neuchâtel, Pinot Noir
Handkäse	beer, cider, apfelwein
Havarti	dry light whites, lager
Herve	full-bodied reds, Cornas
Kashkaval	light dry whites, beer
Leiden	Beaujolais Villages, strong dry whites, gin, beer
Liederkrantz	powerful reds, Rhônes, Riojas, beer
Limburger	full-bodied reds, Châteauneuf-du-Pape, beer
Livarot	Morgon, Calvados, cider
Manchego	Rhône reds, Riojas
Maroilles	Champigny
Mascarpone	Moselle, light sweet whites
Monterey Jack	Chardonnay, light whites, dry reds
Mozzarella	Chianti
Munster	Gewürztraminer, Pinot Noir
Mycella	strong full reds
Olivet	Gigondas, Morgon
Parmesan	Chianti, Lambrusco, Sangiovese
Pecorino	full Sicilian reds
Piora	Pinot Noir
Pont l'Evêque	Corbières, Côtes du Roussillon, cider
Port-Salut	white Rhône, Fronsac reds
Raclette	dry whites, Savoie Blanc, Fendant, beer
Reblochon	Beaujolais, Muscadet, Chablis
Rollot	St-Emilion
Roquefort	minor Sauternes, Monbazillac, Rhône reds
Royalp	fruity reds, rosés
Sage Derby	strong bitter beer
Samsø	light reds and whites
Serra	Vinho Verde
Taleggio	light reds, Valpolicella, Chianti
Tête de Moine	Fendant
Tilsit	light fruity reds, fresh whites, tawny port, beer
Vacherin	light reds, rosés, Chinon, Côtes de Beaune,
Mont d'Or	Cabernet
Valençay	dry whites, light fruity reds
Weinkäse	Moselles, Rhine whites

Recommended international cheese shops

Denmark
Ostehjørnet
Store Kongensgade 56
Copenhagen
Tel. 01–158521

Ostehylden
Købmagergade 61
Copenhagen
Tel. 01–141548

Ostekælderen
Gothersgade 41
Copenhagen
Tel. 01–136418

Eire
Graham O'Sullivan's
  Delicatessen
11 Duke Street
Dublin 2
Tel. 716643

England
Fortnum & Mason Ltd
181 Piccadilly
London W1
Tel. 01–734 8040

Harrods Ltd
Knightsbridge
London SW1
Tel. 01–730 1234

Paxton & Whitfield Ltd
93 Jermyn Street
London SW1
Tel. 01–930 0259

Wells Stores
Streatley
nr. Reading
Berkshire
Tel. (0491) 872367

Finland
All branches of:
Elanto
Oy Sokos Ab
Oy Stockmann Ab

France
Androuet Maîtres-Fromagers
41 rue d'Amsterdam
75008 Paris
Tel. 874.26.90

Creplet-Brussol Fromagers
17 pl. de la Madeleine
75008 Paris
Tel. 265.34.32

La Ferme Saint Hubert
21 rue Vignon
75008 Paris
Tel. 742.79.20

La Maison du Fromage
62 rue de Sèvres
75007 Paris
Tel. 734.33.45

Germany, Federal Republic
Alois Dallmayr K.G.
2 Dienerstrasse 14
8 München 2
Tel. 21350

Italy
La Casa del Formaggio
Via Speronari 3
Milan
Tel. 800858

Salumeria Peck
Via Spadari 9
Milan
Tel. 871737

The Netherlands
De Kaashut
Postjesweg 95
Amsterdam
Tel. 124457

Fromagerie Européenne
Beethovenstraat 37
Amsterdam
Tel. 799037

Kaan's Kaashandel
Koorstraat 11
Alkmaar
Tel. 133455

Norway
Jomfru Hammer's Kjøkken
Frognerveien 6
Oslo 2
Tel. 44 94 00

Sweden
Åhléns
Klarabergsgatan 50
Stockholm
Tel. 24 60 00

NK
Hamngatan 18–20
Stockholm
Tel. 762 80 00

Switzerland
Globus
Löwenstrasse 37
Zurich
Tel. 221 26 10

United States
Cheese of all Nations Inc.
153 Chambers Street
New York, N.Y. 10007
Tel. 732-0752

Ideal Cheese Shop
1205 Second Avenue
New York, N.Y. 10021
Tel. 688-7579

Paprikas Weiss
1546 Second Avenue
New York, N.Y. 10028
Tel. 288-6117

Glossary

Acid-curd milk coagulated by lactic acid rather than rennet

Annatto *Bixa orellana*, a West Indian plant that produces a commonly used cheese dye

Beestings another name for Colostrum

Bloom soft downy mould growth on the surface of the cheese

Blue, blue-veined cheeses with internal moulds, usually blue or green, spreading through the paste

Brined cheese cheese ripened in a solution of water and salt

Buttermilk milk left after cream has been made into butter

Cheddaring blocks of curd repeatedly stacked and turned to facilitate draining and mat the curd particles

Coagulation the clotting of milk by rennet or lactic acid

Colostrum the first milk produced by a cow after calving

Cooked after coagulation the temperature of the whey is raised above the renneting temperature (see p. 6), thus 'cooking' the curds and producing a harder, drier cheese

Coryne bacteria the reddish-brown smear that develops on the surface of washed-rind cheeses

Evening milk milk obtained from an animal during the evening milking

Eyes another word for the holes in some cheeses

Farmhouse made on the farm, usually from unpasteurized milk

Flora the mould growth on the surface of cheeses like Camembert

Fresh unripened

Lactation period the period during which mammals secrete milk

Lactic acid acid produced when milk sours

Lactose milk sugar

Macerated cheese cheese steeped in alcohol and sometimes mixed with herbs and spices

Monastery cheese cheeses invented and traditionally made by monks

Morning milk milk obtained from the animal during the morning milking

Pasta filata a method of cheesemaking that involves immersing the curd in hot water or whey and kneading it until it becomes elastic and malleable

Paste the interior of a cheese, the part that is eaten

Pasteurization a method of partially sterilizing milk by heating it (see also page 5)

Penicillium candidum the fungus responsible for the growth of white surface moulds on Camembert-type cheeses

Penicillium glaucum responsible for the veining of Gorgonzola

Penicillium roquefortii responsible for the veining of Roquefort

Plastic curd synonym for *pasta filata*

Propionic acid its action during ripening produces the holes in holey cheeses

Raw milk unpasteurized milk

Rennet a coagulant usually obtained from the fourth stomach or vell of an unweaned calf, sometimes from other animals, occasionally from plants

Rennet-curd milk coagulated by rennet

Skimmed milk from which the cream has been removed, thus lowering the fat content. Milk may be fully or partly skimmed

Spun curd synonym for *pasta filata*

Starter a culture of lactic acid bacteria added to the milk before renneting to increase its acidity

Surface-ripened cheese ripened by surface moulds

Vell see *Rennet*

Washed-rind cheeses that are regularly bathed in water, brine or alcohol during the ripening period producing characteristically reddish bacterial surface smears

Whey the liquid separated from the curds in cheesemaking

Whole milk with all its fats intact—in other words not skimmed

Index

Page numbers refer to main entries for each cheese;
italicized numbers denote other references.

Acknowledgements

The Author and Publishers would like to thank the following
people and organizations for their invaluable help:

Abbey Farm (Shropshire), Agrexco Agricultural Export Co. Ltd., The
Arab-British Centre, Embassy of the Argentine Republic, Stephen Arloff,
Atalanta U.K. Ltd., Australian Dairy Corporation, Austrian Foreign
Trade Office, Austrian Institute, Dra. Manuela Barbosa, Belgian
Embassy, Joseph Berkmann, Brazilian Embassy, Embassy of the People's
Republic of Bulgaria, Canadian High Commission, Crowson & Son Ltd.,
Cuisine Magazine, Danish Dairy Board, Royal Danish Embassy, DMK
Ltd., Dutch Dairy Bureau, Emberton Bros., English Country Cheese
Council, Food and Wine from France, George Foster, Chris Foulkes,
French Dairy Farmers Ltd., Galbani (London) Ltd., Central Marketing
Organisation of German Agricultural Industries, Cilla Gibbs, The Great
Britain–USSR Association, Greek Embassy, Hungarian Embassy, Ice-
landic Embassy, Italian Institute for Foreign Trade, Catherine Jackson,
Katsouris Brothers Ltd., Lorraine Major, Milk Marketing Board, Ernesto
and Miranda Mussi, National Dairy Council, Royal Netherlands
Embassy, New Zealand Dairy Board, Auguste Noel Ltd., Norway Trade
Centre, J.M. Nuttall & Co., Paxton & Whitfield, Major Patrick Rance, Lizz Rawson,
Caroline Schuck, Brian and Irene Smith, Spanish Chamber of Commerce,
Spanish Embassy, Spanish Institute, Stilton Cheesemakers' Association,
Swedish Embassy, Swiss Cheese Union, Valio Finnish Cooperative
Dairies' Association, Venezuelan Embassy, Dr. Gerta Vrbova.

We should also like to thank the following for their kind permission to
reprint the following extracts: pp. 21, 25 from *The Epicure's Companion* by
Edward & Lorna Bunyard, J.M. Dent & Sons Ltd; p. 51 from *Savage Paris*
by Emile Zola, Granada Publishing Ltd; p. 77 from *Amorgos* by Nikos
Gatsos, tr. Edmund Keeley and Philip Sherrard; p. 87 from *The Epicure's
Companion*, 'The Child as Epicure' by G.B. Stern, J.M. Dent & Sons Ltd.

Special thanks to Farmhouse English Cheese, Camisa Fratelli and Paxton
& Whitfield, London.